2020 Vision

Business Transformation
Through Technology Innovation

Hossein Eslambolchi, Ph.D.

SILICON PRESS
Summit, NJ 07901, USA

www.silicon-press.com

Silicon Press
Summit, NJ 07901
USA

First Edition

Printing 9 8 7 6 5 4 3 2 1   Year 10 09 08 07 06

Printed on acid-free paper.

Library of Congress Cataloging-in-Publication Data

ISBN 0-929306-39-2

Eslambolchi, Hossein, 1957-
2020 vision : business transformation through technology innovation/Hossein Eslambolchi.
p. cm.
1. Management information systems–Planning. 2. Information technology–Planning. I. Title.

T58.6.E75 2006
658.5'14--dc22

2006007042

For Fariba, who makes all things possible

ACKNOWLEDGEMENTS

This book is the work of a number of people, all of whom helped bring it to life: Dave Dorman and Bill Hannigan, fine business mentors; Narain Gehani, an editor extraordinaire; Vida Hashemian and Joselyn Holocombe – the most creative design team; Ed Amoroso, Dave Belanger, Mahmoud Daneshmand, Joubine Dustzadeh, Chuck Kalmenak, Pamela Kirkbride, Bob Kostelak, Bob Miller, Chris Rice, Rick Schlichting, Divesh Srivastava, Tom Tofigh and Chris Volinksy – my former technology colleagues at AT&T; and John Castro and Bill Meyers, whose editorial counsel was so helpful. Thank you everyone.

CONTENTS

Introduction   1

1. Our Converging World   7

2. IP – It's Eating Everything   23

3. Sensors – A Flood of Information   37

4. Broadband – Making the Connection   51

5. Distributed Computing
   – Handling Information Overload   65

6. Knowledge Mining
   – Focusing Less on How and More on Why   75

7. Security – Guarding the Network   91

8. The Smart Environment
   – Using Technology to Self-Regulate   105

9. Convergence
   – A New Universe of Services   117

10. A Day in the Life   131

11. Conclusion   143

Afterword
   2020 Search Technologies   165

Introduction

Being a CIO is one of the toughest jobs in corporate America today. Indeed, the average tenure of a Fortune 500 CIO is less than two years.

Why? Because the CIO must place risky, big-dollar technology bets on an unknowable future. Because the CIO has to understand and work with unproven technology that often takes much longer to integrate and install than originally forecast. And because the CIO's technology choices must cut costs and generate revenue simultaneously.

All this – aligning technology to meet the business demands of cost-containment, customer satisfaction, and compliance as well as coping with the explosion of new products and services – must take place in near real-time.

And the environment is tough, too. Markets are disappearing, combining, cannibalizing. Your workforce needs to be retrained, redistributed, or disbanded altogether. Factories and plants are closing, and jobs are disappearing. It's overwhelming, sometimes even a little paralyzing.

Clearly it's a complex, stressful, and challenging job. And it has become more so in recent years because of the even greater demands that are being placed on the CIO.

So how are we doing? Study after study shows that, by a two-to-one majority, technology executives feel they are getting bad grades from their bosses despite unprecedented productivity fueled by technology.

The need to retain and gain market share today exceeds any one person's scope, no matter how talented they are.

And enterprises across all industries are not simply tweaking their business models – they're being forced to engage in radical top-to-bottom reengineering. Which explains why IT is central to business transformation. And why CIOs and the networking infrastructures they run are central to meeting the challenge of ongoing transformation.

Responses to increased competition range from the automation and outsourcing of key processes to the integration of internal systems to enable the bundling of products from different divisions.

An example of this would be for a company to collapse unproductive silos and move decisions to the areas best capable of making them – based on data, rather than where they have historically been made. Improvements to customer service would include customer relationship management implementations, self-service solutions, security enhancements, and mobile technologies. The success of mergers and acquisitions would then rest on the integration of systems, networks, and processes. And compliance requirements relating to internal controls would spark major change programs to overhaul systems and processes throughout enterprises.

This book examines in depth how new and emerging technologies such as services over IP (Internet Protocol), radio frequency identification, distributed computing, sensor networks, and grid computing can be applied to help today's "new model" CIO drive results to the top and bottom lines of his or her enterprise – thus ensuring the success of the enterprise in the twenty-first century. In essence, it offers a technology vision for 2020.

Why a fourteen-year technology vision? First, with deep thought and with some degree of accuracy, a vision for the year 2020 is possible to articulate. Second, if I go back to 1990, fifteen years before writing this book, cellular technology was in its infancy; PCs were just starting to penetrate deeply into the home; hardly anyone had heard of the Internet, and almost no one used instant messaging or email. Yet all those technologies were in early deployment or on the horizon, and were known to the technical community.

It is the interconnection, the networking, of these technologies that will be the driving technological force over the next fourteen years; it is this convergence that motivated me to write this book. I want to provide a technological road map and imagine a world that moves us from 2006 to 2020, describing what the future will look like and the technologies that will get us there.

We will also explore how these technologies layer, one on top of the other, to bring us to the converged world, starting from current, real-life technologies and building to the future. And finally we will look at how CIOs can work to make our converged future desirable and ethically responsible.

I want to inspire you to embark on your own transformations. I want you to think deeply and strategically about convergence, about its impact on your business and the world around you. I want to give you a context and a way to frame change so it seems less daunting. I want you to see what's coming so you can adapt to these accelerating changes by adding intelligence to your network technologies and making them responsive to the call of new generations.

If your company becomes successful through the application of these ideas, not only will you and your enterprise benefit but, more important, so will consumers and society as a whole. In the end, this book is about the future. I want to leverage my experience as a technologist and as a businessperson to help you understand more than what's coming next. I want you to know how we're going to get there, and how you can position yourself and your company smartly along the way.

I have felt the pain and seen the profit in the transformation firsthand as the chief technology officer of the largest telecommunications company in the world. In leading the transformation of its technology, I learned quite a lot about how aligning the company's business objectives created the opportunity to better serve customers' demands. In the process, both the company and its markets were simultaneously revised.

The key was a commitment to *convergence* – a term I will discuss in detail in the first chapter. I want to share what I've learned on my journey to encourage you in yours. I hope to provide you with a context and a method of framing change so that it is fixed on its outcome, not undone by its implementation.

"Bringing together a massive amount of raw data – from every conceivable place and channel – and transforming it into actionable business intelligence is not just our greatest challenge. It's our greatest opportunity. We're also bringing together our people – customers, partners, suppliers, and employees – to collaborate real time, over every type of device, from the most far-flung corners of the world."

— *Brian Bonner,*
CIO, Texas Instruments

Chapter 1
Our Converging World

Convergence is the buzzword for CIOs these days, but it's not a new phenomenon.

In the second half of the twentieth century, when operators still sat at a switchboard routing calls by hand, telecommunications companies were beginning to use computers to do the job. This was an early example of convergence: telephone technology converging with computer technology to create a far more efficient and inexpensive service.

Today, with the pace of convergence accelerating, the effects are more dramatic.

Inventory systems track products down to the precise shelf; must-have items move to the front of the store the day after buzz hits the Internet, and sales spike. Commodity investors trigger transactions based on minute-by-minute meteorological analysis from half a world away. Services that meld converged technologies like voice, data, video, and text into a single device are growing exponentially. Convergence is affecting *every* way we communicate, collaborate, and do business, and it all looks blissfully automatic to the average user.

If only we were so lucky.

As technology becomes more powerful, smaller, easier to use, and more ubiquitous, the effects of convergence become more widespread – and more acute. It's overwhelming, sometimes even a little paralyzing.

But CIOs who harness this power will generate massive opportunities now and enjoy enormous advantages later. Great challenges engender great successes. Many remarkable corporate transformations – think Cisco, Intel, or Dell – aren't happening in spite of convergence, but because of it. And if you understand convergence, you can be its master and not its victim.

There's no one definition of convergence that's correct, but here's a helpful one:

> *Convergence (n): the rapid and inevitable unification of many disparate technologies into one seamless and ubiquitous global network*

The definition reveals a bias: that networking is so basic to human nature that any definition of convergence inevitably leads back to networks.

The Three Types of Networks

The first step in understanding convergence is to understand networks, and so we're going to take a little time to review some network basics. As elementary as it may seem, once you have the network models in mind, you can start to identify – and harness – converging technologies for your benefit.

So, first, a little history.

Networks are the tools we build to make communication easier. Whether it's about the birth of an emperor or the birth of a business plan, we use networks to spread the word. We expect networks to deliver an answer, even if it isn't always what we want to hear. We'd be lost without networks. In fact, they're part of what human beings are. Our bodies themselves are networks, the concerted cooperation of many disparate organic elements. Billions of cells communicating sensations through our nerves to our central processors – our brains. The intelligence that manages and directs these corporeal networks, in turn, can communicate with other entities – humans, animals, machines – within larger networks of which we are only a part.

To facilitate this communication, we spend enormous amounts of time and energy building networks into our world. And while they've become more and more efficient, they still follow three basic network models that are as old as humanity itself.

First, there are **broadcast networks**. A baby listens as a parent or caregiver transmits information or gives a command. The baby listens, receives praise, or gets information, even if it can't yet talk back.

We use one-way networks to transmit crucial information to a wide base of users. Fire beacons alerting towns to an enemy invasion, a town crier announcing a public execution, a muezzin announcing the traditional call to prayer, a fire alarm summoning a community response, or the simple act of reading a book: all are means of distributing information or instructions from a central location. The best modern examples of one-way networks – television and radio – are now becoming old-fashioned. A central broadcasting tower throws a signal as wide as it can. TVs or radios within range receive the broadcast, but don't return a signal. It's an efficient system, but not very interactive.

The next-simplest network model is a **conversation network**. As a child matures, she begins to have two-way conversations with many different individuals. She exchanges information through language and gesture.

A modern example of a conversation network is the telephone network. You pick up the phone, dial a number, and speak with any other network user who has a device. This network model can be traced back to more primitive technologies, like the telegraph or walkie-talkie.

Finally, there are **community networks**. We communicate with many people at once, and we develop relationships with individuals as well as groups of individuals. We marshal these relationships to procure resources or organize action – from a government task force to a reading group. Culture – encompassing politics, business, art, law – is a vast, complex community network that connects us fluidly to our fellow citizens and to our human past. Sometimes we have a hard time seeing community networks for what they are, because we aren't just using these networks – we're inside them.

Word of mouth is the most basic community network, and a good low-tech example is the postal service. But the most familiar – and increasingly ubiquitous – high-tech example of a community network is the Internet, which allows the efficient creation of communities on a vastly wider scale than any technological community we've ever had before. (More on this in a moment.)

How to Measure Network Power

All this talk about network models and history may be theoretically interesting, but why is it important to you as a CIO, here and now?

Business brings together tens of thousands of suppliers and millions of customers from around the world into a complex series of interlocking networks – and the power and effectiveness of these networks can be quantified mathematically.

Understanding how to measure network power can be very helpful. Let's consider how we can analyze network power using a few simple equations.

The broadcast network is a one-way communication system, and it is only as powerful as the number of people who can listen, whether they are using their ears or an antenna. If you add more devices – more children or more TV sets, let's say – you have a more powerful broadcast network. The power of the network (p) = the number of network users (n). **We can express this mathematically as $p=n$.**

When we move to the next level of network complexity – when network users are allowed to communicate one-on-one with one another – we make another leap in power. In a conversation network like a telephone or a fax network, the number of possible interactions grows exponentially with the number of users. If there are six users, each user can communicate in five possible ways with another network user. The complexity of the network is of order *(n) squared*, where *(n)* is the number of network users. **We can express this mathematically as $p=n^2$.**

Finally, in community networks like the Internet, the number of possible exchanges includes communications between groups of users. A group can be any size, from one user to the whole network. The power still grows exponentially as you add users, but it expands much, much faster than a conversation network. The power of the network (p) = 2 to the power of the number of network users (n). **We can express this mathematically as $p=2^n$.**

You can see that the power of each network type grows as we add users. But adding just a few users to the community network causes it to outperform broadcast and conversation networks at an astounding rate.

The more flexible, interactive, and community-oriented your networks become, the more power each user adds to the network.

Mind the Gap

So, mathematically, network power can be measured and analyzed. But what's the practical application for business?

It's very simple. In fact, it's a mantra that I repeat over and over again: *Business models are network models.* Every aspect of your business is a network. Your services are networks, and your customers are network users. Your company culture is a network, and your employees are network users. And your supply chain is a network; you and your partners are network users.

In order to deliver for your company – to deliver on the crushing demands of revenue, risk-management, and cost reduction – you need to find ways to exploit latent communities of interest in all your networks. Your business is only as powerful as the networks that make it up. And if they're not as powerful as they can be, someone else will seize the advantage. You must transform your networks into community networks now, instead of later.

And you can measure the time you have to pull it off.

In the earliest stages of growth – with the fewest network users – a broadcast network is more powerful than either the conversation or community networks. Add a few more users, and the conversation network is outperforming both the broadcast and the community networks. But add just a few more, and the community network is outstripping both of its competitors – and never looking back.

The power of any community network always begins as far less than that of its predecessors. It starts growing slowly. Adoption takes time, and the older networks have the inertia of growth behind them. But very quickly the community network catches up, matches, and then outperforms its predecessors.

Once the conversation network's power matches or exceeds the power of a broadcast or community network, the game is over. It's too late to transform; you'll always be playing catch-up (if you're still playing at all).

You can apply this analysis to any area of business – from internal communications, to marketing, to inventory, to the supply-chain, to the services you offer. If you leverage the power of community in any of these networks or offerings, your business will become far more effective. And the sooner you do it, the more likely you are to beat your competition to the punch.

As a CIO it's your job to mind the gap. Or gaps. How many different networks in your company can be revitalized and transformed so that your company is operating at full throttle?

Three Lessons in Transformation

Take the example of a telecommunications industry giant of which I was CIO. By the turn of the twenty-first century, it had become abundantly clear that the company needed to change dramatically. Revenues for its traditional market – voice services – were falling. Revenues for its data services were beginning to skyrocket. Those numbers reflected a burgeoning community – a community driving up data traffic.

Unfortunately, however, it was still perceived in the industry as an anachronism. When people thought about it, they thought about its bare-bones network – a series of pipes and ports, really just plumbing for voice traffic and conversations. The real excitement was elsewhere – and this added up to a diminished future for an industry heavyweight.

But the company's exploding data traffic made me and my colleagues pause. How could we exploit it as an opportunity? How could we become more than a conversation enabler? There was growth in that, but it was limited to n^2.

The company needed to make a very basic, very difficult transformation. Its network was a given. It was the largest conversation network of its kind and the company's greatest physical asset. But we needed a technology vision that took it to the next level – to the kind of growth that only communities can engender.

In other words, the company needed to transform itself from a conversation network to a community network. How did we do it?

Lesson one: We optimized our internal communities. When I became CIO, there were seven regional network operation centers. Customers had as many as five hundred different contact points for sales and service. There were more than sixty product silos, each with its own billing, provisioning, and ordering system. And the corporate structure was built around what I call a United Nations model: There were far too many people with veto power. There were multiple CIOs and CTOs for each business group. Positive changes couldn't be made. Decisions were deferred, efforts dragged on, and the time between order and delivery for our customers got longer and longer.

The solution was to create an integrated management concept. This sounds easy, but it is very hard to make it part of an organization's culture. We consolidated our business networks into one centralized location. This allowed us to apply best practices culled from across the company. Product groups became one network – expanding the community and increasing its power.

This management concept is now programmed into the cultural DNA of every employee and embedded into how the company designs, develops, and implements its products. It went from an industry dinosaur to a tightly integrated but flexible community of interest built around delivering service to its customers.

Lesson two: We created communities of interest among our technological systems. Prior to its transformation, many of the product lines and services the company offered each had their own billing, provisioning, and management systems. There were hundreds of disparate systems to manage. And when customers wanted to buy more than one product, this system fell apart. The company needed better integration on its own side to deliver the best service possible to its customers.

We bound our communications and technological systems into intelligent networks that put customers first. We built a single, enterprise-wide architecture for all ordering, billing, and provisioning. We automated every human-to-human and computer-to-human interaction we possibly could. The result: We reduced cycle time between customer order and delivery to a third of its former length. Three years after beginning the transformation, we had achieved the industry's highest customer satisfaction rate.

Lesson three: We expanded out service offerings. Finally, we turned to our customers, offering them value-added services based around communities of interest. We decided we wouldn't limit our offerings to a well-run conversation set of pipes and ports, but instead create application architectures designed to expand customers' community interests by merging their own networks with their customer and partner networks. The company introduced services that intelligently distribute resources depending on the changing needs of the customer's applications. And it expanded its investment and commitment to Internet Protocol (IP) services.

The company changed from a plain old network service into a software-based networking solutions company.

The Future of Networks

This book isn't just about sharing my views with CIOs and offering advice on running a business today. It's about preparing for tomorrow and the 2020 vision. And as I look forward to the future, I see an extraordinary change coming – within the next fourteen years, in fact.

The simpler forms of networking – broadcast networks, conversation networks – will be absorbed into the fabric of one grand community network. Every bit of information – every interaction – that was formerly delivered by these networks will be delivered by one community network, the Internet.

Many people have written about the transformative power of the Internet – how it makes the world smaller, more efficient, more connected. All this is true. But what is truly transformative about the Internet is that it will absorb all other means of communication. On the most mundane level, we can see today how radio broadcasts, television programming, movies, and telephone conversations are all beginning to be transmitted over the Internet. This is the true hallmark of its transformative power, a distinction that many people, even technically savvy people, miss.

It's not that television shows will disappear, or that the phone call as we know it will become obsolete. It's just that the traditional means of delivering these communications will vanish, folded into the fabric of the most powerful community network the world has ever seen.

Billions of devices, from temperature sensors to clock radios to cars to supercolliders – connected over extreme broadband to powerful distributed processing, storage, and decision-making systems – will create, in the next decade or so, a convergence of communities of *technological* interest. They will cooperate, gathering resources, performing actions, forming and reforming according to want and need. And they'll do it faster and more powerfully than traditional human community networks ever could before.

The possibilities of active participation are still hard to imagine because the technology is so new – and because we're so used to fifty years of regular one-way television. One model that shows the possibilities is massive multiplayer online gaming. The players design their own characters – and determine the flow and outcome of the storyline.

In the future, we'll collaborate with other people watching the same programming. People will work together to design their own movies, with the story and ending they decide upon. Just as the Internet brought unlimited choices, now choice will spread to other areas. Because it's open and nonproprietary, people will be able to plug in and collaborate with one another. These capabilities will depend on networks that are smart – in order to support a wide variety of smart devices and a wide variety of applications.

These layers of technology will wrap intelligence around all our familiar environments – our homes, our cars, our markets and theaters and cities. We will live, fully immersed, within communities of interest that are wider and more powerful than any we have ever known. The future of your business rides on the creation of this grander, richer global network.

Never before has *one* medium promised – or threatened – to subsume every other medium. **And this transformation is the cause of the disruptions you see every day in your business, and in the world of communications as a whole.** It is, quite simply, the cause of convergence. There's an ancient Chinese curse: *May you live in interesting times.*

Times couldn't be more interesting for the CIO.

The Future of Business

How do you stake out your place in this rapidly converging world?

Luckily, the driver of convergence – Internet technology – isn't just the harbinger of massive disruption. It has a beneficial side, too. The Internet is the ultimate community network, and if you prepare to leverage Internet technology now, it will allow you to navigate transformations in the present and into the future with much greater ease.

Intelligent service-centric computing will help CIOs continue to attune themselves to deal with the unpredictable, and become more business- focused. I believe it is the end users' behavioral changes that will impact CIOs. As technology advances, and new solutions are adapted by consumers or businesses, we will witness cross-usage behavior models between consumers and businesses. As end devices become cheaper, smarter, and more powerful, the same multifunctional end devices will be employed for both business and personal use.

Your network will have to be fluid. As we move toward the converged world of 2020, networks will include a greatly expanded set of participants, including customers, employees, vendors, and physical items and sensors. All these individuals will participate in your network, and the networks of your competitors, engaging and disengaging from each with blinding speed. You'll need to secure, monitor, measure, track, collect, analyze, and maintain all the critical data and transactions among these participants operating on a bewildering variety of end devices. In a world where almost every device will communicate over the Internet, you need to be prepared to leverage as many of these devices as possible to provide the best service to your customers. You need to create flexible, open network structures now that can handle these changes later.

Your network must be thoroughly IP-enabled. Let no legacy system survive! We'll see later on in the book why every aspect of your business networks will benefit from being IP-enabled, but for now I want you to consider that changing your legacy systems to IP will be far less painful now than it will be later on. And since most wireless systems are IP-based, you will have to convert to IP eventually. If you do, your services and products will have the flexibility and extendibility that your customers will require in an increasingly mobile world. The next generation of access networks will be required to support a wide range of services, including mobile broadband Internet, high-quality voice and broadcast video, sensory services, and security and surveillance.

Discover what technologies to bank on. Follow the money. You may be humming along fine with systems that have served you well for years, but make sure that significant investment is still being made in the underlying technology. If you notice that capital is being invested in an upstart or competing technology or system, start looking toward making the switch yourself. Even a service perfectly tailored to your company's needs – a service backed ferociously by your own techies – may be hopelessly isolated and out of date in ten, five, or even two years. As we move towards the year 2020, we are in effect introducing intelligent service-centric evolutions through smarter networks and more sophisticated end systems. As end user behavior changes with technology advances, new solutions adopted by consumers and businesses will witness cross-usage behavior models between consumers and businesses. With end devices becoming more powerful, users will be enabled with multifunctional converged capabilities (see Table 1). Watch the investment community, and watch where it's spending its money. If you do, you can make necessary changes *ahead of the curve.* You'll stay competitive and get in on the bottom floor of the next technical revolution.

Leverage your expertise. While most CFOs feel like they're spending too much money on IT and networking already, these disciplines are *absolutely essential* to business productivity. CIOs must, of course, collect, analyze, and visualize the data that will allow operations to make informed choices about how to run the business. Is the new IM system for your sales representatives yielding bottom-line results? Does customer cycle time peak because of particular geographic or call-center factors? This type of information makes IT a key player in operations.

This is just the start of our trip, a moment to map out our course and acquaint ourselves with a few guiding principles. The mission of this book is to explore how we'll reach the converged world – layer by layer, step by step, technology by technology. We'll document this transformation from today to the year 2020, and as we explore each step we'll suggest how you can be prepared for the journey.

	End-user behavior (Worldwide)	CIO Concerns	Impact
2005	• 35% cell phone usage • 35% use emails • 15% use laptops • 35% use Internet • 10% IM • Digital camera for consumers • MP3 player (new generations) • HDTV infancy • IP telephony is in infancy • Push to talk	Multidimensional DNA • IT Investment • Security • Storage • Cost optimization • Network BW • Information sharing • Prepare for unexpected • Eliminate shaky foundations • Massively scalable • Manageable • Adaptive (speed, Structure)	Beginning of multimedia era
2010	• Broadband wireless • Push to view, • Peer-to-peer comm. • Multimedia handheld • Tablet PCs • IPTV • Natural language interface	Seamless Access • Decentralization • Adaptive to unpredicted conditions • Applications usage/ utilization • Security of their mobile users • Enable e-collaboration • Digital rights management • Backup mobile devices • Always on connections • Closer link with partners and suppliers • Government compliance • Clean up the legacy systems	Ubiquitous broadband

Table 1
Convergence Through Technology Evolution

	End-user behavior (Worldwide)	CIO Concerns	Impact
2015	• Internet-enabled objects • Petabytes of storage • Enhanced unstructured search engines • Location-based services • Sensory networks	Knowledge portals • Provide life-size virtualization experiences to their customers and employees • Optimize network usage models • Knowledge of management tools • Meta-data signaling • Customization/ maximize opportunities • Manage service relationships	Personal broadband Personal intelligent robots
2020	• Fully converged networks • Personal broadband/ personal intelligent robots • Virtual societies • Seamless natural interfaces for all	Common language for all • Adapt to changes, new ways to interact • Control intellectual assets • Privacy laws • Managing mobile networks • Identity management • Collaborative thinking	New ways to deal with financials, health care, transportation, Education, business interactions, entertainment. Email, laptops, IM, existing phones almost a history.....

Table 1
Convergence Through Technology Evolution (contd.)

FUTURE PREDICTION

IP will be used for more than 95% of all global communications traffic by 2020.

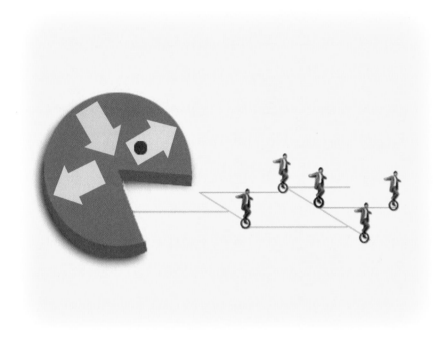

Chapter 2
IP – It's Eating Everything

In the 1980s, before the Internet came of age, a breakout video game called Pac-Man, in which a tiny electronic creature gobbled up everything in sight, captivated the country. These days, Internet Protocol (IP) is behaving like Pac-Man, engulfing every service, every application, every device. And the growth of IP services is destined to continue.

Over the last fourteen years, the estimated volume of traffic over the Internet has expanded 100,000 times over. Of even greater significance, the number of end points on the Internet has increased 32 times over – or, interestingly, 2^5 times over, echoing the mathematical growth of community networks we discussed in the last chapter.

At this rate of expansion, IP will be used for more than 95% of all global communications traffic by 2020. Almost all electronic devices will have wired or wireless IP interfaces. The ubiquity of IP in network communications will enable plug-and-play devices that seamlessly communicate with each other regardless of how they are connected, or where they reside. Users of IP devices will be able to connect easily with IP networks anywhere in the world.

What's driving this expansion? The term *autocatalysis* is helpful. If, in any process, the conditions are just right, every step forward results in an intensification of the conditions that caused the process to begin in the first place. That's what happened – and continues to happen – so spectacularly with the Internet. With each passing day, new devices that leverage IP go online – and these devices are becoming smaller, more mobile, and more potent at every step. So the community of potential IP users grows. As a result, IP carries more content to more devices, which in turn encourages more people to adopt IP, and this calls for ever-smaller, more mobile, and more powerful devices.

An Object Lesson in the Power of Community

While the continuing expansion of IP now seems inevitable, it got off to an uncertain start. In its earliest forms, IP was a highly flexible protocol, but it emphasized ease of transmission at the expense of service reliability. At first, information technology professionals placed their bets on ATM – the asynchronous transfer mode packet protocol. At the time, ATM handled voice and video much more efficiently than IP, was far more secure than IP, and seemed to be the natural choice for expanding electronic services. It was touted as *the* solution for connecting large networks of mainframes. But because ATM was designed to accommodate so many services, overhead was very high – effectively excluding small personal computer users in the burgeoning PC market.

The seismic force of personal computing, combined with the explosion of the Web, doomed ATM. The new, rapidly growing PC community demanded an easy and low-cost way to network, and IP fit the bill. ATM wasn't cost-effective for small users. And because the PC community was expanding so quickly – and the community of high-end mainframe systems wasn't – IP eventually superseded the high-end protocols.

Had ATM focused on providing *widely distributed service* instead of designing the technology around as many services as possible, it might have become the protocol used across the Internet today. But it was overdesigned. ATM was designed for high-end systems. It was designed to handle challenging services like video and audio well, rather than simply communicating efficiently and easily. And the Internet approach is to get something simple out, and then iterate. ATM didn't do that. With 20/20 hindsight, the lesson from this experience is clear: Adapt your technology to the services users want. And always keep your eye on the needs of the community.

Evolving IP

IP technology has since evolved to match or exceed ATM's capabilities. The emergence of multiprotocol label switching (MPLS) in the 1990s, for example, allowed IP to approach the same level of quality of service that ATM networks had achieved. MPLS allows IP to mimic the way ATM and similar packet-switching protocols guarantee reliability.

The problem with early IP networks was that while they would attempt to ensure timely packet delivery, it wasn't a priority in the same way it was for ATM. The delivery route wasn't chosen in advance or managed by a central authority. Packets bounced from router to router, and they often arrived incomplete or with significant delays. On the other hand, ATM networks guaranteed the reliable transmission of data by determining, at the beginning of any packet's trip through the network, the most efficient and safest route for the data, and sticking to it.

MPLS, in turn, was designed to help IP networks create similar "dedicated" routes for IP packets. Furthermore, MPLS enables IP networks to choose the best routes for data on the fly. If there is difficulty anywhere along the preferred route, MPLS adjusts by suggesting the next most efficient path. This has tremendous implications for online commerce: IP's flexibility combined with MPLS reliability creates powerful business service possibilities.

Transaction processing is at the heart of most CIOs' concerns. Take a simple credit or debit card swipe at a retail store. Every swipe needs to be handled reliably and securely, or the company will lose business. And because of IP's early history, many people are still reluctant – in 2005! – to convert from point-to-point transaction systems to IP processing. But now that MPLS offers reliable and secure connections, it is crucial to make the move to IP. Why?

IP systems allow a multicast of data in real time. In a point-to-point transmission, the data from any one sale gets sent straight to a computer at company headquarters for processing. Once it's done, the computer transmits the sale data to various partners and departments for action. But with IP and MPLS, the same sale data can be transmitted securely and, most important, simultaneously to your marketing department, your supply chain partners, your inventory management systems, and so on. Information on product popularity, stock levels, and supply-chain availability are actionable on the fly, leading to far tighter integration of your business networks. IP enables community growth.

Imagine harnessing eBay-like environments for companies with tremendously complicated ordering and provisioning challenges. Online auctions put community growth at the center of their business models. These same forces are latent in your supply chain and other partnership. All you have to do is unleash them. Why not create an eBay-style auction environment that unites your supply and distribution chain automatically and instantaneously? These are the types of opportunities that IP and MPLS open up for any enterprise. (We'll talk more about this in Chapter 3, Sensors.)

Additionally, the convergence of IP and MPLS is crucial to advanced services involving audio and video streams. Real-time services like voice transmissions and webcasts need more than just high bandwidth. These services depend on reliable end-to-end communication. Traditional IP networks – without the reliability guaranteed by MPLS – could drop or misorder significant amounts of data. If half your audio stream takes twice as long to arrive as the other half, how can you have an efficient webcast or video conference? The obvious answer is, you can't.

Convergence – From IP to VoIP

However, harnessed together, IP/MPLS networks can create enormous possibilities for converged services. Furthermore, because IP is compatible with a wide variety of access technologies used in a network (Ethernet, wireless, fiber, multi-service edge, etc.), it can deliver services to a wide range of users. Services no longer have to be built for the specific network access technology that any specific device is using at that particular moment.

Likewise, the reliability guaranteed by MPLS allows a multitude of services to be built "on top" of IP networks – everything from email to streaming video. Yet IP has retained the simplicity of its structure. This combination of different service types and customizable communications leads to a staggering array of possibilities. The end result is that by providing a stable standard in the middle of the telecommunications hierarchy, IP changes the whole service arena.

Let's examine a present-day example of a service that's driven by IP convergence. Voice over IP (VoIP) offers significant enhancements over traditional voice services, many of which are the by-product of the convergence of several different technologies.

For starters, the convergence of voice into data improves service quality. As VoIP matures, its transmission quality will become *much* higher than today's traditional phone network. The steady growth in processing power in end devices combined with advances in data compression technology will enable the delivery and speedy processing of extremely large amounts of data. This data can then be dedicated to the quality of the voice stream itself, which will soon reach CD-quality levels.

Besides, convergence offers other valuable service enhancements. VoIP allows you to create call routing and voice mail applications that don't require special switches or reprogramming of your telephone network. New applications that didn't exist before also become possible. As speech recognition and automatic translation technologies improve, for example, you'll be able to index and search your voice mail – as you are now able to do with email. There are already services that integrate voice mail and email, allowing you to receive and listen to them simultaneously.

Consumers have already embraced VoIP and are driving its growth. But businesses are also migrating their operations to VoIP – because of price, and because of the value-added services and capabilities it allows them to deliver. For example, cable companies are moving hundreds of thousands of users to VoIP, part of a "triple-play" strategy that offers voice, television, and Internet services at significantly lower prices than each service separately. We will see companies applying VoIP to their networking infrastructures to deliver applications and features in an increasingly converging market of consumers and end-users.

At the same time, we are witnessing an unprecedented battle for voice customers: telephone companies are competing for their traditional customers against other large companies that are trying to lure them away. This has helped lower price boundaries for global voice communications. Indeed, when voice is routed over IP, international long-distance charges are drastically reduced if not eliminated altogether. Making a call internationally may soon be as inexpensive as dialing locally. Call centers of every stripe are becoming VoIP-enabled so that dialing a local or a toll-free number may connect you with someone halfway across the globe.

VoIP is clearly a transformative converged technology that offers significant benefits for corporations and consumers alike. By 2020 VoIP won't be an option for voice telephony; it will be the standard – as ubiquitous as the copper wire is today. And just as with the adoption of any converged technology – as we mentioned in the last chapter – moving to VoIP helps enhance competitiveness.

Media Convergence Beyond VoIP

But IP convergence delivers much more than voice traffic. Any service – not just voice communication – can be provided over IP, leveraging its speed, efficiency, and flexibility. We've already witnessed the revolution in streaming video and audio. Radio stations now broadcast over the Internet. Video streams carry news from around the globe to your browser. Music and movie downloads, television broadcasts, video conferences – all of these services are converging over IP and becoming commonplace. You can harness this convergence to change the way you do business. Indeed, you'd be making a colossal blunder if you didn't do so.

Say, for example, that your company has secured a big contract far from any of your established field offices. You need to set up operations and get your employees on the ground and up and running as soon as possible. In the past, it might have taken weeks or months to locate the proper facilities, order equipment, and ensure the reliability of networking solutions in the office. The power of IP will change all those calculations. IP convergence will allow you to plug one device into a broadband network to instantly meet all your communications needs.

You will be able to set up an office instantly in any location with a broadband connection. Such a device will interact with VoIP devices and the network to arrange for an instant telephone presence. More important, it will supply a WiFi signal to all your company's devices, allowing them to network with each other and the home office. You'll be able to receive voice, video, audio, email – *any service* – wherever you are. Your communications will be converged over one connection and tied to *you* – not to your home or business telephone lines or your laptop or desktop. You can take the device with you wherever you need to go, and still maintain the same business presence and capabilities.

Services, personal preferences will follow you wherever you have access to broadband, and adapt themselves to the devices you have on hand. In fact, they'll be integrated with your office communications and will adapt to your schedule and location, filtering various communications if you are at home, on a business trip, or on vacation.

All the ways that you connect to your colleagues, friends, and family will become seamlessly integrated, too. Cell phones, for instance, will be able to move between VoIP networks, wireless networks, and traditional cell networks without the user ever noticing a change – a huge boost for reliability and range of use. Different communications services, like instant messaging or text messaging will be integrated with voice so that if you drop a call, or need to remain quiet in a conference room or at home, you can continue your conversation over text as a natural extension of a phone conversation. Communications will be *built around the user*, instead of the user having to adapt to her devices.

This community network transforms all communications into data – recordable, searchable, storable, manipulable data. In turn, this opens up enormous possibilities for future service offerings. In the coming years, IP will support all sorts of converged services, including conferencing, training, entertainment, and especially gaming, a huge and growing online industry. But we're getting ahead of ourselves. We'll be discussing IP-enabled services throughout this book, and particularly toward the final chapters when we see how these services will change the way we live in 2020. But for now, let's concentrate on how a company – like yours – can position itself to offer innovative services when the opportunity, and the desire, arises.

Innovate What You Know

Desire, of course, is the mother of invention. When it comes to offering your company and your customers innovative, converged services, you and your co-workers have plenty of great ideas. The difficulty is that they're always based around what you *can't* do right now: I wish my supply-line partners could peer directly into my inventory. I wish my sales reps could search through every product offering our company has and index them against updated offerings from the competition.

The fact is that you and your co-workers are natural innovators, because you're constantly thinking about what you would like to be able to do but can't. Dave Belanger, an industry colleague, has a favorite saying: *The guys who design the best games play games all the time.* They want to create gaming features that are faster, cooler, and more dazzling than any they've experienced before. Because they know the limitations they're faced with, they have a user's desire to transcend them.

The same rule applies to business. The people who dream up innovative conference-call features spend a lot of time on conference calls. Innovative ideas about inventory and supply come from people who are preoccupied with inventory and supply. If you want to offer converged services to consumers, your ideas will come from your daily experience. Conversation has existed since the dawn of mankind, but think about how the telephone changed its shape. Furthermore, think about how instant messaging is changing telephony now. Each of these technological advancements has filled a gap or satisfied a need.

Transforming ideas into reality, of course, is about more than having the desire in the first place. Engineering your ideas is the next step, and responsible engineers are trained to make the improbable possible. Can we make the idea happen? If we can, how do we do it? To hit the innovation "sweet spot" you need to set up a culture in your department that combines the best in wishful thinking with practical, hard-nosed engineering. Ideally, you should be fostering innovators who understand both the service side and the engineering side of the equation.

IP Meets the Future

At the moment, it truly seems that IP is opening up an almost limitless number of service possibilities. An increasing number of devices – smaller, more mobile, and more powerful than their predecessors – are fueling existing IP growth, guaranteeing an even more robust future. And that's the problem.

The current version of IP, version 4 (IPv4), was designed twenty years ago to connect millions of computers. But the millions of computers that once used IP are rapidly turning into *billions* of computers, devices, and sensors. IPv4 won't be able to provide them all with addresses.

So IP itself must evolve.

Enter IP version 6. Instead of the several billion possible addresses provided by IPv4, IPv6 will provide 340 trillion, trillion, trillion addresses.

But IPv6, which will become the standard version of IP, doesn't just offer more room for technology to grow. It also offers improved security over IPv4 by classifying traffic within the individual packets. This allows devices to identify and direct packets according to specific security policies, a feature missing from IPv4. IPv6 packets also contain information that identifies the origin of the packet, helping ensure further data integrity and network security. With 256 bits of information in every address (as opposed to IPv4's 32 bits), IPv6 helps make cryptography far more effective.

There are already several projects under way providing platforms for the testing and development of IPv6 applications and technologies. Organizations are creating their own IPv6 programs – including the University of New Hampshire, which houses a special laboratory for technology standards; the Third Generation Partnership Project, the Internet Engineering Task Force's working group on 3G wireless, which mandates the use of IPv6 in all 3G devices; and the Department of Defense, which has mandated that its networks run over IPv6 by 2008.

The Department of Defense is not alone. IPv6 requirements are increasingly being embedded into the bid requirements of government agencies, which demand the highest levels of security, reliability, and reach because of the nature of the customer – the U.S. government.

The first challenge the transition between IPv4 and IPv6 presents is adoption. The move will create a burden on individual companies. Before a company can leverage the full power of IPv6, it will have to purchase devices and systems that are compatible with the new version. This will incur significant costs and, for technology professionals, it requires significant planning.

But should you get ready to move to IPv6? The answer is an unambiguous "Yes." And when should your company do it? As soon as possible. Why? Because the entire network – from core fiber pipelines to the lowliest network router – is moving in that direction, and you don't want to be left behind. And the longer you wait, the more tedious and costly the transition becomes.

Like any network technology, IPv6 increases in power very rapidly as it gains more users. We saw how powerful this growth can be in the first chapter. So while the value of moving to v6 will seem low to moderate for a while – maybe for a few years, although probably less than that – increasingly it will become a big problem if your company is still reliant on IPv4. And it isn't just about limited address space.

In fact, address space for your company alone is *not* the issue. If you're running an enterprise network behind a network address translation

(NAT) router, you're likely to have enough address space for all your enterprise devices for quite some time. But eventually you'll need to communicate with large-scale networks outside of your enterprise – like the Department of Defense, for example. NAT routers and non-v6 equipment will tend to interfere with many services that will be performed over IPv6, such as VoIP. You could create hand-tooled solutions for communicating with these services, but why waste the time and money creating specific solutions when you can adopt IPv6 now and avoid the problem?

Likewise, network equipment manufacturers will be slowly phasing out IPv4 and phasing in IPv6 to their products. Eventually you won't be able to get support or even replacement parts for your IPv4 networks. Procrastination will likely lead to greater costs and more problems. The longer you wait, the less time you'll have to manage the conversion properly. That, in turn, will probably increase – not decrease – your overall technology costs.

One More Challenge ...

One other significant challenge remains, and for the time being it's something the CIO has very little control over. Who will control the structure of the network itself? Internet technology was born in the United States, and for years now regulatory organizations in the U.S. have exercised de facto control over the Internet and its development. But the concerns of regulators and business in the U.S. are not the same as those in other countries – most obviously nations that place a premium on strict control of information.

So suppose you're the CIO of a global enterprise. If pressures from different telecommunications rules in China, for instance, begin to encroach on your services, you'll have a major headache moving information back and forth over the "border." The structure of the network is quite uniform, but this may change as time goes on. From censorship to taxation, many countries and organizations are focusing, however slowly, on changing the network structure. Unfortunately, questions surrounding the international control and structure of the network are almost impossible to answer right now. Predicting a likely outcome is well nigh impossible. Nevertheless, it's clear that international political and policy developments will have an important influence over the future shape of the network.

But just as progress's forward march cannot ultimately be stopped, neither at this point can IP. IP is the bedrock of the converged world of 2020. Trillions upon trillions of IP addresses will inevitably create fascinating opportunities.

Any person, place, or thing can – and indeed, might – become an element in the burgeoning global network. We will develop into an IP-centric society, dominated by human information systems, networks and, as we'll explore in the next chapter, the sensors that feed information to these networks.

"Integrating sensors into the network has the potential to transform entire industries. More and more, we see companies utilizing sensors to tap into vast new sources of data, unleashing a depth of intelligence never before accessible to them. Sensors are making smart networks smarter, and transforming good companies into great ones."

— *Marv Adams,*
Senior Vice President
of Corporate Strategy and CIO,
Ford Motor Company

Chapter 3
Sensors – A Flood of Information

Over the next decade or so, we will witness one of the most dramatic changes in the amount and timeliness of data regarding all aspects of our world. This will come in the form of sensors – literally trillions of very small devices with the ability to record information about themselves and their environment.

Networks, whether human or technological, are designed to communicate information from one point to others. But the value of a network is largely dependent on the information it contains. And so the sensors that feed information into a network play a crucial role in maximizing its value. The better the sensors and the better the information they provide, the more valuable the network becomes.

Our most fundamental sensors, of course, are our senses themselves. They are quite sophisticated, the product of a complex evolutionary design. And yet we've improved on them as time has passed: telescopes and microscopes extend our eyes, thermometers extend our touch, and satellite dishes extend our ears. In addition, virtual sensors have been used for many years to monitor our computing environments. But now, thanks to ever smaller, ever more powerful computer processors, sensors will soon be small and inexpensive enough that they will be everywhere – from the stock shelf to the fault line to the apartment-building lobby. And with the advent of trillions and trillions of IPv6 addresses, they can all be networked. This massive distribution of networked sensors will create orders of magnitude of more data than our networks and systems have seen, and allow us to create better information, more quickly than we've ever had before.

But the omnipresence of sensors also means that computer networking will undergo a radical shift. Instead of separate, distinct entities, networks will become a seamless part of the larger environment. And this creates unprecedented new possibilities. For starters, we can begin asking more precise and useful questions – about the nature of earthquakes, the preconditions of a mining disaster, or the efficiency of the power grid, to name but a few examples.

In turn, this momentous shift generates immense opportunities for business. Armed with more and better information, managers can collaborate with broader communities of interest – their staff, their customers, their partners – far more efficiently, intelligently, and competitively than ever before. But it presents immense challenges as well, particularly for the CIO, not only charged with creating and maintaining the architecture of this bold new world, but also with harnessing the ever increasing amount of data so that it can be used efficiently and intelligently.

Revolutionizing Medical Study

Today there are over 25 million mice sold a year for science research and study. Imagine the difficulties that we go through to measure the animals' behaviour under different drug tests. Cataloguing the subjective results and developing a proper conclusion can take years.

Injected sensory chips which can memorize and report animal behaviors continually are about to change the entire medical research industry: sensory-enabled nano-machines will provide not only a great deal of localized intelligence, but also a wealth of information that can be useful when aggregated in the data-mining centers. Application of sensory-injected monitoring nano-machines will be applied to humans for detecting and distinguishing a simple cold from a flu or epidemic conditions. Linking this information to medical network-connected intelligence and databases will create a wirelessly linked environment where nano-machines can adapt, cooperate, and optimize themselves in concert with other intelligent machines.

In campuses and hospitals we will witness the installation of first-generation wireless sensory networks consisting of small, intelligent, low-power nodes capable of sensing, processing, and controlling; communication will be a collaborative process among all members and control centers.

The next-generation sensor networks will be autonomous, intelligent, and mobile. These sensors will reconfigure themselves to achieve certain tasks. These requirements will provide rigid requirements for the computing, and delivery systems of 2020. The networks and computing systems must reorganize themselves to serve the distributed agents with needs to communicate and exchange decisions, actions, and knowledge to other agents in secured environment.

The RFID Revolution

Let's start with one of the most significant sensor success stories: radio frequency identification (RFID).

At this moment, there is over a trillion dollars' worth of commercial goods circulating around the United States. Assume that just 1% of that is lost, damaged, spoiled, or stolen each year. By labeling every product, every pallet, every container, and every shelf with IP-enabled sensors, you can track your entire supply chain or inventory immediately and transparently, and claim your share of that 1%.

RFID is the labelling system behind IP-enabled inventory and supply. Standard RFID tags contain three times the amount of information that can be stored in barcodes. They transmit data without contact or line-of-sight with the reader, and can be read through dust, snow, ice, paint, or grime – conditions that render optical technologies, like bar coding, useless. Long-range tags can be read at speeds achievable by cars or trains – E-ZPass, FasTrak, and other automated toll readers are a good example of this.

At the moment, most RFID tags are "read only" and passive. With a virtually unlimited operating lifetime, they consist of little more than a computer chip and an antenna. A compatible reader provides power to the tag over short distances – between a few centimeters to thirty meters. The tag "awakens" and reports any information it has available to the reader. Active tags, on the other hand, are self-powered, have longer ranges than passive tags, and are constantly reporting relevant information to any reader within range. Active tags are becoming increasingly common, especially on expensive items, or cartons of items. A reader installed in a Panama Canal lock, for example, can automatically receive information from active tags in every vessel and shipping box that passes through. Additionally, some RFID tags are writeable as well as readable.

You've probably seen these tags being used by FedEx deliverymen. The reader writes information to the tag: the location, date, and time of scan and condition of the package.

An Internet of Things

RFID technology grew out of an industry-funded laboratory at MIT, and it shares some similar characteristics with IP. IP is a remarkably flexible addressing system for information while RFID is a flexible addressing system for physical objects – any tagged item can be identified in countless useful ways. RFID creates "an internet of things" – a world of objects connected by Internet technologies. Indeed, it's possible that this new internet of objects could significantly affect network architecture in the years to come.

Recognizing its potential, Wal-Mart was an early pioneer of RFID, embracing it as a tool for reducing inefficiency and pumping up productivity. Partly with the help of RFID, Wal-Mart is looking to reduce its industry-leading inventory turn from forty days to even lower levels. And now autocatalysis is kicking in: not only are more and more retailers using RIFD, but its use is spreading to other related industries as well. No company wants to be left behind and presumably suffer the consequences.

In turn, the number of applications in which RFID technology is being used is greatly expanding.

- Officials at the European Central Bank, for example, have been working on a project to embed RFID tags into higher-denomination euro bills. (Reports that the United States is doing the same thing are, so far, unsubstantiated.)

- The Dutch Library Association has created an RFID standard for all its member libraries that allows the automated check-in and check-out of books, accurate inventories of library assets, and the automated reordering of missing books. This reduces costs and frees up library staff for other duties. One result: Dutch publisher NBD/Biblion is embedding RFID tags in the 27 million books it produces annually.

- Chase Bank is now offering MasterCard and Visa credit cards with embedded RFID tags. Testing on the Chase program has shown a twenty-second reduction in checkout times with the new RFID-enabled cards. And users perceived an increase in security – because the card never leaves your hand. MasterCard, American Express, and Visa are actively encouraging many other retailers to adopt this technology as well.

Indeed, any business environment where loose items of value need to be tracked with a high degree of accuracy can benefit from RFID technology.

Sounds almost magical, doesn't it? But the promise of RFID technology obscures the real work is involved in its implementation. Of all the challenges faced by the CIO in today's complex corporate environment, this one could be the most daunting.

Step one is developing an appropriate network of readers, edge servers, and back-office support systems. Where does your work flow intersect with new information? Is it important that the information attached to the object be updated? How much information do you want to record? Do you have the bandwidth to handle the increased upstream data traffic? Do you have enough storage space to hold all this information, both at the retail level and at the home office? Are your employees sufficiently trained to manage these networks? If not, what service provider can support such widely distributed systems? Finally, you'll need to share this data with your vendors and your customers. Are your systems compatible? How can you ensure that you're sharing only the data you want to share? Is the data secure?

These are all very tough questions, and adopting RFID is a very big investment. If you don't answer these questions accurately and realistically, much of the crucial information you gather will go to waste.

Once you've tackled these fundamental issues, you face another crucial decision: Do you want to build and run an RFID network yourself, or can you perform these tasks more quickly by leveraging the expertise and assets of an outside vendor? If you're serious about RFID, you'll need networks that keep in step with the amount of information you're going to be harvesting.

Beyond RFID

Of course, RFID sensors are still in their infancy. In most cases the information that needs to be placed in the RFID tag is still entered by a human operator (like the FedEx deliveryman) using a writer/reader. But more advanced sensors that report directly about their physical environment will enable truly revolutionary applications. Already there are sensors that can detect, measure, and transmit any physical quality – temperature, pressure, color, shape, sound, motion, chemical composition. And, as sensors are becoming more sophisticated, they are also shrinking in size. Some are so tiny that they are difficult to detect.

At the same time, as you would expect, sensor networks are growing in size, depth, and sophistication. Recent advances have led to the emergence of wireless sensor networks, consisting of battery-powered "motes" with some computation and radio communication capabilities. Advancing wireless technologies will allow these sensors to be embedded into almost any conceivable location. And revolutionary mesh network design will help bolster the flexibility and durability of these distributed sensor networks. Cooperating mesh network devices form networks on the fly, intercommunicating with one another, allowing some or all of the sensors or devices on the network to act as a router. One or more of the devices function as gateways to the Internet, giving all the nodes in the network access. These advanced networks can be maintained, even if some of the end points are lost. So if you deploy enough devices with mesh capability, you can create a far-flung chain of network access, allowing connections in areas where it is hard to place transmission towers, admittedly at the expense of added network delay.

This convergence of technologies – tiny sensors, IP addresses, wireless communications, advanced network design – will be able to produce very precise, very accurate assessments of the state of any environment. It's really impossible to catalog all the possible applications of these converged sensory networks. But a few scenarios can give you an idea of just how profoundly these applications will affect the way we live over the next decade.

Consider health-care applications, for example. By 2020 molecule-size sensors will be able to monitor and report on body chemistry, allowing doctors to possess a complete analysis of the body's environment in real time. This in turn will allow for more highly targeted medications that respond to the body's fluctuating chemistry, helping to maximize individual treatments and minimize the side effects of various therapies. Indeed, it's possible that in the future every patient will receive a subdermal read-write medical sensor that contains his entire medical history, updated with every visit to a health-care practitioner. These sensors will be easily read by any emergency room doctor or nurse anywhere in the world. Since it will be possible for all patient information to be collected as part of one larger network, hospitals will be better able to monitor the overall state of public health – keeping better track of, say, the spread of infectious diseases or the consequences of a biological terrorist attack.

On a more global scale, sensors will also be used to monitor – in far more sophisticated ways than are now possible – the state of our environment. The widespread use of environmental sensors can help address persistent questions about the effect of pollution on nature and wildlife. We'll be able to learn more about the effectiveness of environmental "therapies" designed to reintroduce endangered species or clean up large-scale toxic spills.

And we'll be able to better protect our food supply, as well. Sensors will alert us to bacterial contamination and other potential threats. Researchers at the Universitat Autònoma de Barcelona have already developed miniature sensors to help detect food poisoning and other contaminants in our food. These sensors use DNA to "feel" out the existence of diseases like salmonella or botulism. The sensor DNA's connection with the bacterial DNA generates a slight electric current that alerts scientists to the presence of the contaminant. Traditional tests for the presence of salmonella require several days; the Barcelona DNA sensors can identify it within several hours. More important, it can do so in many different places in the supply line, ensuring greater protection. Sensors can also be used to protect our water supply. During the summer of 2005, researchers at Syracuse University began testing robotic sensors in reservoirs and lakes in New York State to monitor the purity of the water. Other universities are planning similar trials.

Sensor technologies are revolutionizing authentication procedures for security systems. One fascinating example is face-recognition technology, which uses video cameras to sweep crowds for possible troublemakers at public events. The camera produces a video of a crowd, and is then able to analyze each face, examining each individual's bone structure, which can be as revealing as an individual fingerprint. Other face-recognition technologies can already scan a 3-D "sculpture" of the human face with such accuracy that it can differentiate between twins. Indeed, the days when criminals and terrorists can disguise themselves to avoid arrest may soon be over.

Upcoming advances in construction materials will allow sensors to be embedded within critical structural points. When industrial or natural disasters occur – an earthquake, say, or the undermining of an office building by construction work in an adjacent lot – sensors can report the location and vectors of the damage without costly (and dangerous)

invasive investigations of the structural framework. Engineers, public safety officers and urban planners can learn the exact condition of the structure and efficiently target repairs. Emergency personnel responding to a collapsed building will be able to determine the likelihood of rescue without endangering their own safety.

And the list goes on. It's possible that sensor technologies will allow cars to have built-in collision-avoidance capabilities by the year 2020. A sensor-enabled reader in a computer or entertainment device could detect whether a CD or DVD is an authentic or a pirated version. Even if there is no immediate application for sensor technology within your enterprise, there is bound to be in the future.

Of course, sensors alone won't bring about these changes. Just because you have received data doesn't mean you know what to do with it. We'll discuss the hardware "intelligence" necessary to create advanced sensor data applications later in this book. The key point is that deeply embedded sensor networks will make computer-assisted decision-making and collaboration an increasingly important part of the fabric of our everyday lives.

An Orwellian Nightmare?

Will sensors and related technologies be a force for good or evil? Inevitably, any discussion of sensor technology raises concern about individual privacy. George Orwell probably wasn't the first to raise this point, but his description of a totalitarian state in his book *1984* is the one that vividly evokes the issues raised by privacy advocates, civil libertarians, and others. In the novel there are sensors everywhere. Microphones are hidden in apartments, in offices, even in the woods. Cameras monitor every possible interaction. Most ominous of all is Orwell's predicted use of television: signals are broadcast and received in two directions – and the sensors can never be turned off.

So how close are we now to this Orwellian vision becoming the reality?

The act of monitoring environments, in and of itself, isn't a threat to privacy. In fact, more often than not, it's a boon to both privacy and security. Security cameras already routinely protect our homes and businesses. The advanced face-recognition technology discussed early can just as easily protect our privacy, as violate it. The larger point is that it isn't really sensors that cause most privacy problems. We tend to attribute far more power to sensors than they actually have.

Nevertheless, there are ethical, political, and technological steps we can take to address these privacy concerns. For instance, sensors can be programmed to be disabled. Another possibility is to mandate that sensor design incorporate certain precautionary features. There could be different types of sensors, just as today we have different top-level domains for IP addresses. The design specifications would be different depending on the intended use. Sensors for business uses would differ, say, from those uses in law-enforcement and military applications. Each would have strict limits on the type of information they could gather and who could retrieve it.

Inevitably, sensor technologies – and their use in monitoring environments – will be subject to government regulation and industry oversight. As they should be. The important step in ensuring privacy in our sensor-enabled world will be an ongoing, evolving discussion about what rights we wish to guarantee, and to what degree we can and will protect them. Technology is value-neutral. It's the role of government and its citizens to make the appropriate distinctions.

An issue more vexing than privacy – especially for CIOs – is likely to be whether companies have the bandwidth to deal with all the information being generated by the explosion of sensor technology.

If, for example, Wal-Mart is able to reduce its inventory turn below forty days with the use of RFID technology, it would be processing, storing, and analyzing over one hundred times as much information as it dealt with previously. CIOs have to concern themselves with making sure that their companies have the bandwidth to carry the coming flood of sensor-generated information.

And the first swells of the information tidal wave are coming into view. We've seen how RFID already holds the promise of revolutionizing the way physical products are moved, managed, and maintained. Video and audio devices (e.g., webcams) are small enough and simple enough that an average home computer user can distribute them around the house. Of course, these same devices have been deployed in corporate environments for quite some time. Over the next several years, all these sensors will become dramatically cheaper, smaller, and more easily networked. Though any one device – even a video device – delivers data in the few-megabit-per-second range or less, the aggregate will create a flow of information that easily exceeds the content on current backbone networks.

Today there are IP networks that can carry 2.5 petabytes (that's 10^{15}) of traffic per day. They manage in real-time streams of data that generate hundreds of billions to trillions of bytes per day, and generate databases in the several-hundred-terabyte range. By 2012 sensor-originated traffic alone will be on the order of 4,000 petabytes – or 4 exabytes. The good news is that this is a stunning source of real time, valuable information that will lead to competitive advantage for those who are ready.

But companies and CIOs will need to plan ahead – way ahead – to be in a position to take benefit from this data explosion and the competitive edge it offers. The next chapter will delve into how to transmit the tsunami of data that is washing over us.

FUTURE PREDICTION

Within a year the trunk lines at the core of the fiber network will be operating at speeds of 40 gigabits per second (Gbps); by 2020 they may support speeds exceeding 640 Gbps. In addition, by the year 2020 we will provide 1-Gbps intelligent pipes to homes and businesses.

Chapter 4
Broadband – Making the Connection

Broadband connections are the nervous system that relays information gathered from sensors to us. Fat trunks of optical fiber feed down into smaller connections to the office and home. Fiber-optic lines are the spine, Ethernet cables or additional fiber serve as ancillary nerves, and a variety of smaller pipes – from T3 lines to cable, DSL, and dial-up – connect distributed sensors across the whole network.

As we saw in the previous chapter, the content that is coursing along broadband connections will be driven by an explosion in sensor data, as well as all the secondary data that will be created in the process of analyzing and manipulating that information. In fact, it's quite likely that the data we generate to manipulate data from sensors will outstrip the amount of the original data. And while there's already a huge quantity of information flowing over the network, in the years ahead, it's only going to continue to grow.

The demand for higher broadband speeds is being driven by other factors, too. Moore's Law states that the number of transistors on a square inch of silicon will double every eighteen months, essentially saying that processing power will double for a fixed price every eighteen months. By that measure, devices – from desktops to laptops to PDAs – that are placed in the hands of consumers are likely to achieve processing speeds of up to 20 gigahertz (GHz) by the year 2020, almost ten times the power of today's average consumer laptop. All this extra processing power will make possible increasingly rich, instantaneous multimedia applications, driving up broadband speeds even further. To match these needs, networks will have to provide bandwidth at a rate of one gigabit per second to consumers.

But there's no immediate danger that our technological nervous system will suffer a breakdown. Within a year the trunk lines at the core of the fiber network will be operating at speeds of 40 gigabits per second (Gbps); by 2020 they may support speeds exceeding 640 Gbps.

Now let's consider "access bandwidth" – the much smaller pipes used by consumers and small businesses to connect to the Internet. Access bandwidth is crucial, because it's the edge of the network, the points at which the consumer or the small businessperson plugs in and receives services over IP. Currently DSL, the most popular broadband service, offers speeds of up to 3 Mbps. But that still doesn't match the speeds that the multimedia network of 2020 will require.

We need a new name for the speeds we want to achieve. The present generation of broadband (cable, DSL, 2.5G wireless) will prove insufficient to carry many of today's advanced applications. Currently, broadband services such as DSL and cable – operate at a bandwidth greater than 2.0 megabits per second (Mbps). But when we start talking about speeds over 1.2 Gbps to the edge of the network, the only appropriate term is extreme broadband, or XB.

The Last Mile – Wired Solutions

The "last mile" of network connectivity has been plaguing the telecommunications industry and its customers for a long time. Increasingly sophisticated and powerful business and consumer devices are demanding more and more bandwidth from telecommunications networks. But these devices are generally located in offices or homes that have limited bandwidth access to the network.

In the recent past, the fastest broadband access available for the home or small office has been DSL and cable. Each represents a vast improvement in speed over telephone access dial-up service. But DSL and cable still run over copper phone wires and coaxial cable connections and, while faster than telephone lines, they, too, have their limits. Neither provides the speeds to meet the growing demands of today's businesses and consumers.

How do we solve the last-mile problem? How do we bring high-speed XB connections to the edge of the network?

One solution is to extend the high-speed wired network itself to the business or the home. This is referred to as FTTX – fiber to the x, where x represents homes, businesses, neighborhoods, etc. FTTX will deliver XB service with the same reliability as T1 and T3 lines, which most companies use today. Considering that video streaming requires only 4–6 Mbps, there will be more than sufficient bandwidth available for Internet, cable TV, Voice over IP, and other yet to be invented services. This is the critical benefit of FTTX. FTTX enables advanced multimedia and data-intensive services down to the home and the small office, facilitating the deployment of new, decentralized office structures (such as office-in-a-box ™, which is discussed in Chapter 2).

But there are significant barriers to this FTTX solution. As we well know, running fiber to homes and businesses requires a lot of capital outlay, work , and negotiation. Streets and other structures may need to be dug up or otherwise altered so that the fiber can terminate at or near a home or business. Additionally, significant investments in infrastructure technology are required to manage sending fiber signals to a large number of locations.

The Last Mile – Wireless Solutions

Enter wireless fidelity (WiFi) and worldwide interoperability for microwave access (WiMAX), two other possible solutions to the XB issue. WiFi enables broadband wireless communication over local areas. WiFi hotspots are connected directly to wired high-speed Internet connections, and are capable of routing Internet traffic from over one hundred WiFi-enabled devices at once. One WiFi coverage area can reach about a hundred feet to devices, and within that range now offers connection speeds of 54 Mbps and even higher soon. Its initial use is within buildings and limited outdoor environments. This limited range best favors local mobility, since so many cells need to be set up to cover large areas.

WiMAX, in contrast, allows for high bandwidth over longer ranges. Thus a combination of long-range WiMAX antennas and short-range WiFi antennas can provide complete indoor and outdoor last-mile broadband service for metropolitan areas or large business or government facilities.

Another promising wireless access technology that is nearing deployment is free space optical communications (FSOC). FSOC uses lasers to transmit data through the atmosphere. To date, there are no wireless-spectrum licensing requirements or government regulations governing its use, which, as you can imagine, is a big plus. FSOC can deliver up to 2.5 Gbps of bandwidth and may, over time, deliver much higher speeds. While FSOC is a line-of-sight technology and has some limitations – dense fog can block transmission and shut down the network for longer links, for example – it will be part of last-mile solutions as the technology matures.

Wired or Wireless?

Both wired and wireless broadband are achieving popularity as last-mile access solutions and both have their strengths and weaknesses. FTTX and wired solutions are good for multiple applications that can require very large bandwidth, while wireless access solutions allow real-time, mobile applications that need less bandwidth. As is so often the case, the solutions that emerge may be determined as much by politics as technology. Some municipalities and local government have been providing citywide wireless connections as a public service at very low cost. Legal battles between municipalities and telecommunications companies over the right of local governments to install their own broadband services are already under way. The good news for consumers and businesses, however, is that a technological solution is in the offing.

Convergence of Wireline and Wireless Networking

Whatever access technologies ultimately prevail, there are other crucial issues that need to be addressed. Expanding the network requires a network architecture that is flexible, can incorporate many different access technologies, and can work seamlessly with the current wired network structure. Your company doesn't want to worry about which device it should use or where and when it can or can't use it.

The most promising development in this sphere is 4G wireless broadband, wireless IP-enabled networks. Because 4G networks are IP-enabled, they fully and easily interconnect with a wide range of individual devices, a capability that earlier wireless technologies – like Local Multipoint Distribution Service (LMDS), for example – lacked. This allows enormous flexibility for on-site business communications. Many different mobile devices – such as laptops, tablets, and PDAs – can be used interchangeably by a wide variety of distributed employees. These devices are in the process of replacing traditional telephone services as business communication tools, and 4G helps make them even more powerful.

4G wireless architecture uses a tiered or mesh approach to wireless networking. Towers in metropolitan areas transmit signals, which are, in turn, delivered to other wireless base stations. This architecture is meant to serve small businesses, office buildings, business and residential users. Each tier handles quality-of-service and class-of-service issues for traffic appropriate to its area. This type of network structure ensures efficient and reliable network service to almost any location.

Additionally, a 4G wireless network mirrors similar bandwidth pipes in the wired network, allowing the wired infrastructure to be leveraged for the back-haul or metropolitan access portions of the wireless network. These parallels allow both the wired and the wireless networks to communicate with, support, and draw resources from one another. The bonus to businesses is an enormous improvement in the reliability of wireless service. Interruptions or spikes in use on either the wired or the wireless network can be intelligently rerouted to the nearest available open bandwidth on the other network.

The beauty of 4G wireless networking is that it enables the evolution toward a converged XB service, combining the wired and wireless networks in a ubiquitous, always-available, mobile broadband network. The last-mile problem will be eliminated altogether.

Businesses that are ready to leverage this new environment will enjoy real advantages over their competitors. But making sure that your company is ready for wireless mobility is complicated. It involves intricate migration of users and service hand-off issues, as well as significant investments in equipment and training.

Adopting 4G

So how can a company manage the switch?

The first key question is when to adopt 4G? What are the triggers or opportunities that should signal the right moment?

One important consideration, of course, is cost. If, for instance, your old PBX or private phone system is reaching the end of its depreciated life, it could be cost-effective to consolidate your information networks as you make the move to VoIP services. Alternatively, if your wiring costs of new remote locations or offices are draining your budget, adopting 4G might make economic sense.

And that raises another consideration in this complicated calculus. If your employees are beginning to increasingly work at home, or your offices and facilities are becoming widely distributed, switching might make sense, whatever the state of your legacy systems. The tiered structure of 4G combined with IP-enabled VPNs (virtual private networks) allows an exact recreation of work environments.

Pay attention to the devices your employees use. If they are beginning to favor devices with multimedia integration over PDAs or tablets, for example, 4G is a good bet. One additional caution: Keep your eye out for unacceptably high messaging and paging costs. 4G can help you deliver these distributed services at a lower cost to more varied locations.

The challenge for CIOs and network providers will be the degree of network intelligence that needs to be embedded in their solutions. In most cases, we will witness tightly coupled application controls and signaling with the networks. Our networks will witness more complex data, faster information exchange, and much more interactivity among the users and intelligent objects. Applications will expect broadband bandwidth for multimedia devices in homes and businesses. These applications will always be "on," available, and will provide CIOs with new business opportunities.

As with every new technology, as 4G networks become more widespread and costs for 4G-enabled devices shrink, adoption rates will be driven higher. So keep one eye on your operations and the other on the 4G community, and look for the sweet spot between cost benefit to your company and affordability of change.

Once you've made the decision to switch, you have some other choices to make.

Step one is preparing your physical assets. The infrastructure of your network needs to meet the demands of wireless broadband. You'll need to develop a plan to retire your remaining circuit facilities. In locations where your needs are not met by pricy T1 connections, install WiMAX connections, especially for remote and branch offices. In your existing Ethernet networks, plan upgrades to allow the future expansion of service bandwidth providing high-speed (100–1000BaseT) or faster capability. Likewise, make sure that upgrades to your WiFi devices are fully compatible with all existing standards (a/b/g) and allow for carrier-grade Quality of Service (802.11e) and roaming standard compatibility (802.11r). This will ensure that you get the longest life out of your wireless equipment.

Step two is preparing your networks and services. If any of your legacy applications aren't IP-enabled, reengineer them now so they are. This will allow a seamless interaction between any application and any other application or device. Make sure your existing WiFi systems are equipped with the latest security standards or use a layer 3 VPN. Change your passwords from the factory defaults. As you move forward, choose hardware that supports VPNs, such as IPSec for data and VoIP traffic, and institute company-wide VPN policies so that everyone can work securely and within standardized methods. Choose devices and applications with open source code or open architecture.

The third and final part of the process is grasping the human impact of the change. The knowledge needed to implement all these changes may exceed your in-house IT staff resources. If it does – or even if you *suspect* it does – consider outsourcing network design to better handle integration and installation. In fact, it may be wise to consider a managed equipment service model from a large carrier: the bandwidth and design demands of your business's network will start to approach the operating levels of carrier subnetworks.

A managed service model removes strain and training costs from your staff, freeing them for other tasks; it also leaves carrier-level reliability and availability in the hands of the pros. Finally, ease the transition for nontechnical employees. Make sure there is a grace period where both legacy systems and the new 4G applications are working simultaneously to ease the shock of conversion. Create interfaces that emulate older technologies, like telephone keypad interfaces for VoIP PC applications. Make the most of the multimedia tiger you've unleashed by providing streaming how-to videos and other user-friendly training aids.

The Convergence of Telecom

This coming XB revolution won't just change your business, it will change telecommunications as well.

Take cable, for example. So far, cable companies have had some success competing with local phone companies by offering VoIP, Internet, and television over one cable connection. For the first time in their history – as voice service is being swallowed by IP – phone companies are fighting for their traditional business. But the unique value that cable adds – television programming – isn't safe either. The TV portion of the triple play – voice communications, Internet, and television – will be swallowed by IP as well.

So when all is said and done, the triple-play package will collapse back into a single-play package: Internet access will be king. Phone companies are already responding to cable companies with newer high-speed versions of DSL and consumer-friendly FTTX offerings. Every service will be offered over IP, resulting in a bandwidth price war that will allow extreme broadband speeds to become almost vanishingly cheap.

This, in turn, will change the way broadcasters create and distribute content. The community network fostered by IP disconnects the production of content from the delivery – processes that are very tightly integrated in the traditional broadcast model. This has tremendous implications for the entertainment and news industries.

One good example is radio. There are more than ten thousand radio stations on the Internet today "broadcasting" over IP. Since most people listen to radio in their cars, these IP services are not widely available to them. If, however, the wireless Internet provides broadband mobility to cars, then any of those stations will be accessible while driving. This is transformational, as radios are slowly being converted to IP delivery. Additionally, new devices and delivery systems are already in development to deliver media over converged devices – think of cellphone–iPod combinations, or the video clips available with new wireless phones.

Satellite radio is a proprietary attempt at skirting traditional content delivery while adding more options. But with the coming pervasive 4G network, there will be a better delivery mechanism, with more choices for content – choices that are limited only to the power of the community network.

So while cable TV and satellite radio eat away at traditional broadcasting models, this trend will continue and accelerate. Broadcasters won't be known for their association with particular channels or stations, but rather for the quality and consistency of their content. Content distribution will fall to aggregators who will assemble the material into thematic or localized packages; these aggregators may also provide interfaces for users to customize their own content. (The aggregators may, in many cases, be the Internet service providers themselves.)

Moreover, there will be thousands of choices for multimedia consumers, because the creation of content will be increasingly decentralized. We've already seen this multicasting revolution in dramatic action – the video produced by observers during the December 2004 tsunami disaster, for example. Lightweight, affordable, and high-quality video equipment, combined with the community sharing power of the Internet, decouples production from distribution. Individual consumers will be awash in a multimedia sea, and the hotspots of opportunity lie in editorial aggregation – helping users navigate this sea of content.

If you are a CIO in the content delivery business or in broadcasting, and you know this is coming, how do you adapt to it? You should plan on reducing capital spending for acquiring additional assets like broadcast towers and radio gear. Plan to deliver CD/DVD–quality audio and video versions of your broadcast, leveraging the broader bandwidth over IP for increased quality. Mostly, look at how you can combine with, or become a content aggregator. Perhaps initiating discussions with consumer electronic manufacturers and network providers makes sense. While network, content delivery systems, and devices are still catching up to the demands of high-quality multimedia over IP, we can see them developing on the horizon.

Even if you're not in a traditional content production industry, you'll feel the cascading effects of the multicast revolution. Is your marketing department ready for these new forms of content delivery? Can they adapt to new avenues where consumers are used to little or no advertising at all? Your business – no matter what your industry is – undoubtedly produces enormous amounts of data and, increasingly, enormous amounts of multimedia content. How do you store it and deliver it to your employees, partners, and customers? New multicast production and distribution models can help you recast your internal communications so they're more efficient and flexible. Imagine applying a consumer-based model of content aggregation – organizing content by theme or topic for automatic delivery – to all your internal communications. You can send targeted media packages to everyone in your organization depending on their department, area of expertise, security clearance, and so on.

Finally, the entertainment industry is being shaped by broadband in another, more negative way: Because of the sheer amount of information that broadband connections can deliver, whole films, TV shows, and albums are being delivered back and forth across the Internet. While the Recording Industry Association of America (RIAA), the Motion Picture Association of America (MPAA), and other industry groups have won many legal battles to restrict file sharing – most notably against Napster – they're having trouble winning the war.

Attempts to institute digital rights management (DRM) technologies – designed to reduce or restrict access to proprietary content – have also met with new efforts to copy or pirate that very content. But it's crucial to note that DRM is essential for business in general: for secure and safe communications, as well as for the broad assurance that creating unique content will be economically rewarding. Expect the dance between DRM and pirates to continue for the foreseeable future.

The Broadband Universe

We've seen how broadband is today's most disruptive technology. But in a broader sense, it is a *unifying* technology. Because wireless XB will be ubiquitously deployed, broadband will gradually become less like the branching human nervous system and more like an enveloping environment.

In his book *A Brief History of Time*, Stephen Hawking discusses an early-twentieth-century model of the universe: a cosmos that is continually expanding, but is at the same time limited. Space isn't infinite, yet it has no boundary; it bends back around on itself. If you travel far enough, you will eventually wind up back where you started.

That's what will happen with XB. The XB nerve structure won't end at a "skin" the way the human nervous system does. It will turn into a whole self-enclosed universe, doubling back on itself. You will be within it wherever you go and, what's more, it will always be expanding. If every end point – every device, every machine, and every sensor – is a star point in this expanding universe, broadband will be the space that surrounds them all. And the more this universe expands, the faster the information will travel between users and end points.

By the year 2020 broadband access, broadband applications, and broadband networks will be focusing on scalable bandwidth, trusted delivery infrastructure, and seamless location-based computing and protocol services. Multilayered pipes (VPNs) with sophisticated settings will drive the networks to be tightly coupled with computing and storage infrastructures. The impact of protocol standards and open architecture will be the driving force for acceptance of such technologies by the users, leading to a new era in globalization.

We often say that ours is a "small world." Globalization is only making it smaller. But if our world seems smaller, the information generated to manage it is getting *larger*. And in order to leverage all this growing information usefully, we need the processing power and computing resources that can cope with it. This is why we need what is known as *distributed computing*, discussed in the next chapter.

"To keep pace with the demands of increasingly compressed business cycles – as well as the pressures of unforeseen events – we need technologies that are more flexible and more adaptable. We call this removing the 'friction' from the system – the inefficiencies, the labor-intensive, outdated technologies – and replacing them with flexible, Web-based services."

—*Fred Matteson,*
SVP and CIO,
Fireman's Fund Insurance Company

Chapter 5
Distributed Computing – Handling Information Overload

Through the 1970s and 1980s, telecommunications networks followed a "smart network, dumb device" model. The classic example was the telephone network. The network itself routed the calls; the phones themselves were "dumb." The same held true for most early computer networks. In general, very large computers connected to very small and simple terminals. The terminals were "dumb": they simply entered or reported data from the network.

In the 1990s, things changed. Just as IP helped turn individual islands of networks into a sea of connected computers and devices, designers and theorists began to revise the network model. IP enthusiasts felt that the network itself needed to be dumb – it needed to be a simple conduit between computing devices that could intelligently handle data and services. The ever-growing community of Internet users would receive data and manipulate it on their end.

But both of these models have their problems in today's ever more complex service environment. If present-day devices – from the wireless phone to the PDA to the desktop computer – were mere dumb instruments, we would overload the amount of data being sent over the network, since each device would need specific instruction for every task, every time.

On the other hand, if the device is loaded with intelligence, and the network is merely a simple series of ports and pipes, it creates a whole set of other problems. Consider an IP service that connects many thousands or millions of devices. Each device cannot manage every separate connection between itself and any other device. Thousands of devices – let's say wireless phones, for example – would be forced to carry all the information needed to route calls, store messages, and guarantee call privacy, not to mention connecting the call and letting you talk. It would be absurd. It would also mean very complex wireless phones. A good analogy is a symphony orchestra; to make great music, it's important to have an intelligent conductor who serves as optimizer and organizer and who keeps all the instruments playing in harmony.

Designing a service is like swinging on a pendulum between device intelligence and network intelligence. At one extreme, you run into scalability problems; at the other, performance and reliability deteriorate. As we move toward 2020, the pendulum will have to come to equilibrium, or businesses won't be able to manage the complex needs of their customers.

Today IP-service companies are embracing a network design philosophy that balances intelligence between devices and the network. They consider the service the customer wants to provide and then split the intelligence accordingly. This "split intelligence" distributes resources – from bandwidth and processing power to data and content – where they're needed to provide the best service. They are creating, in effect, a vast computing environment whose functions are distributed over many technologies, and whose resources – including storage – are allocated to many different areas in the enterprise as they are needed. But how do you effectively move toward a split-intelligence system? How – and when – do you implement it within your company?

Computing the Next Move

Distributed computing is, in fact, a lot like chess. You have to compute as many of your opponents' possible moves as far in advance as possible, and see the ramifications of those possibilities before you make your own move. But in this case you're playing against multiple opponents. Facing you across the board are all the vagaries of modern telecommunications. When will there be a spike in traffic? Do we have enough processing power to handle terabytes of stored data? Are our resources being used in the most efficient way? As in chess, strategy is key.

It is now possible to create service concepts that address these challenges. Services that will allow applications that are especially communications-sensitive – that need immediate access to high-speed connections or unused processing, for instance – to be distributed to network environments where these resources are plentiful.

Here's a simple example. You're a retailer and it's Christmastime. Your website is experiencing huge spikes in last-minute shopper traffic, and some of your servers have stopped responding. At the same time, you're tying up valuable bandwidth with a variety of internal business tasks – email applications, perhaps. Using this new service concept, the network can determine that the retail sales applications will get preference over email applications and be moved to a server on the network with a larger bandwidth capacity. They don't have to be run at your facility and communicate out to the network and back again; instead they'll operate on an XB broadband pipeline in your service provider's network, immediately leveraging the bandwidth the provider has at its disposal. When the fluctuations cease, the applications will reorient themselves in the network into the usual configurations. This is movable computing – computing that anticipates your next move. The provider organizes its network around your needs.

But developing this type of service and similar technologies is a set of opening moves in a much bigger and longer game. As time passes, the lines between the network, the devices that connect to it, and the services they offer are blurring.

Using the Other 90%

It is widely believed that human beings use only about 10% of their brain capacity. This "fact" has been in circulation for around a hundred years or so. But it isn't true. No serious neurologist has ever substantiated the claim.

A similar claim is made about computers – that every day, on average, only 5% of Microsoft and 10% of UNIX® server processing power is used, and only 30% to 40% of global storage space is employed at any given time.

This, unfortunately, is true.

It's a tremendous waste of resources, but it's somewhat understandable. We design extra computing power into our systems to handle surges in activity. But these surges are by definition the exception and not the rule. Additionally, computers are usually working on human time. When your business closes at the end of the day, all those resources are still available, and no one is using them. Why are we wasting all these resources? Could we harness all the available bandwidth all the time? All the processing power? All the storage capacity?

The European Organization for Nuclear Research, CERN (originally the Conseil Européen pour la Recherche Nucléaire) – which counts among its many inventions the creation of the World Wide Web – will soon possess one of the world's most sophisticated devices for scientific research: the large hadron collider, or LHC. The collider will smash proton beams against one another at close to the speed of light, yielding ever smaller elementary particles. It will be an important tool for helping us understand the subatomic structures of our world.

The LHC will churn out information on the order of 15 petabytes a year, roughly the equivalent of 500,000 30-gigabyte drives. In order to process all this data, CERN will use a technology known as *grid computing*. Grid computing utilizes unused processing power and storage space across a wide spread of cooperating computers. The amount of data CERN needs processed is so large that it is developing the largest grid-computing system in the world. Its subprocessing sites include international university and research facilities as well as corporate facilities, such as Hewlett-Packard.

Grid systems don't have to be as massive as CERN's. Some grids incorporate thousands of small processors – like desktop computers. Others incorporate distributed computing power from servers, desktops, and business machines throughout a business or an organization. The pharmaceuticals industry uses grid computing to study the action of drugs at a molecular level, for example. Design-based industries (the semiconductor industry and large industrial machine manufacturers) use grids for collaboration design simulations. And they're very popular in the financial services industry as well: Wachovia installed a grid-computing solution that reduced derivatives trading simulations from fifteen hours to fifteen minutes of run time. As a result, trading increased 300%.

There are other telltale signs that grid computing has arrived. Expedited patents have been issued to Data Quality Solutions (DQS), a Silver Spring, Maryland, company specializing in grid architectures. DQS's products integrate data from domestic and international intelligence agencies over one grid architecture, an application that's helpful in combating terrorism. Only ten companies in the last forty years have received expedited patents. Additionally, Microsoft is launching a cluster computing application that manages clusters of up to 128 machines.

When is the right time to look at adopting grid solutions? Obviously, if you're finding a significant percentage of your resources underutilized, it may be profitable to create an internal grid or to join an external partnership. On the flip side, if any one of your applications is threatening to overwhelm a single large mainframe, it may be time to ease the burden on that machine through a shared computing architecture. Likewise, if the combined computing assets of different distributed locations within your overall enterprise are showing under- or overutilization, these locations can be knit together into a grid.

How you go about building a grid is a bit trickier and, of course, depends on many factors that will be unique to your business environment – the type of architecture your systems are running on, the type of applications you need to spread over the grid, and the intensity of spikes and troughs in enterprise-wide processing. First and foremost, however, grid computing is most useful if the applications you want to share are capable of being processed in parallel. If many of your application's key tasks can be crunched at the same time – if the results of one task do not affect or rely on results from another – then that application is more suited for use in a grid environment. You may wish to reorganize applications so that their components can be handled by multiple processors. Additionally, you need to determine if your existing hardware is suitable for grid computing or not. For instance, does your processor interconnect architecture need to be upgraded? Can your separate machines pass data smoothly and efficiently? If there's a bottleneck between processors, or clusters of processors, you may miss out on any benefit at all.

Grid solutions face another possible obstacle. Often nontechnical executives oppose them on the grounds that, depending on the size of the grid you want to implement, they may require you to share resources with other companies and organizations. But just as often there's a strong business case to be made in favor of a grid solution. And there are other potential benefits as well. For example, the processing power you'll gain won't just ease current usage; it will enable uses that were previously unavailable to the company. You'd be well advised to create incentives and policies that reward interdepartmental sharing and promote gains in processing power. And you should train experts within your department who are well versed in the use of grid-enabling technology such as the Globus toolkit, an open-source resource for building grid systems and applications.

If You Don't Need a Grid …

No matter how popular it becomes, grid computing isn't for every business. At a minimum, though, your company will be interested in being tightly coupled with grids because they constantly feed you new knowledge about your business. But many businesses don't have applications that need the massive computing power that grid computing addresses. For these businesses, what's known as *utility computing* may be useful and cost-effective. That said, it's important to point out that all these highly distributed solutions will have to be enabled by sophisticated secured infrastructure, so that the computing takes place across a very secure network fabric.

Utility computing is the leasing of processing power and storage from a service provider. You may lease only one processor from your provider, or you could lease power from a large-scale grid. Either way, utility computing services help your business leverage dormant or underused processing or storage by dynamically allocating resources from heavy workload servers to light ones.

Utility solutions are appropriate when the issues center around cost concerns and departmental efficiency rather than on the complexity of large-scale computing applications. And these days – with IT budgets frequently being slashed – this is often the case. Say your data center needs significant expansion in capability, but the costs are out of reach. Utility computing may be the right solution. Alternatively, if you're developing a crucial application that will have heavy, though unpredictable, spikes in demand from users, utility computing could give you the capacity you need at a more affordable cost. Similarly, if you're moving to an open source architecture or otherwise reevaluating your enterprise infrastructure architecture, utility computing models can help.

You should select a utility pilot program based around your needs. First, benchmark your internal benefits and costs so that you have an adequate measure for the new utility application. Make sure that the benchmarking captures adequate data to measure as many different levels of performance and demand as possible. Armed with this data, select a pilot or pilots that offer solutions to your particular demand cycles. Make sure that you can manage internal barriers to the utility, especially software licenses that may need to be purchased to run on your "extra" utility processors. Allow significant time for the pilot – as much as six months – to get an adequate measure against your original benchmarks.

The Future of Distributed Computing

As time goes on, companies will connect as many of their internally available computers – and all other electronic devices – into massive intragrids. And, as we move toward 2020, companies will begin to connect their own intragrids with intragrids from other companies, creating even more powerful "extragrids." That in turn will spark the development of many massive, worldwide computing grids, using processing power and storage resources from around the globe – formed on the fly.

As we've noted, CIOs will utilize grid computing for managing their digital media assets as well as taking advantage of interconnected servers with cooperative applications. In addition, at the heart of grid computing is the concept that applications and resources are interconnected in the form of a pervasive network fabric that is accessible everywhere and sharable by everyone.

Indeed, grid computing provides the working model of a long hoped for universal distributed computing facility: the giant "world computer" of science fiction. But this will never resemble the sinister supercomputer of *The Matrix* trilogy. Although the largest grids will interconnect, the result will not be one unified machine. The purpose of this supergrid will be simply to provide cheap, and almost infinitely scalable, computing – not to control the world as the computer in *The Matrix* did. In doing just that, however, it may contribute to a future where every user – business and consumer alike – and every application has access to power and storage space similar to today's supercomputers.

With vast amounts of computing power, storage, and intelligent maintenance of network assets available in the near future, advanced collaboration will become routine. But today's distributed computing is just the first step in the design and development of truly widespread collaborative systems. As we move toward 2020, virtual computers will be created on the fly to serve our needs, disbanded when we're finished, and then recreated to serve our needs again. This model, which takes significant programming and planning to execute, will become more and more automated, to the point where much of the work of organizing the collaboration will be invisible.

What's the next ingredient for truly powerful, truly prescient collaborative communities? The more complicated our collaborative needs become, the more intelligence is needed to manage both the data that's shared and the number of users manipulating the data. The next chapter discusses how to bring that intelligence to bear on our collaborative efforts.

FUTURE PREDICTION

Our distributed, collaborative smart databases will utilize technologies such as intelligent search engines, knowledge mappings, control feedback systems, and more to continually learn from the patterns, behaviors, and actions. This will enhance business' information and help execute decisions. By the year 2020, knowledge-mining technologies will dramatically change the way all information is networked.

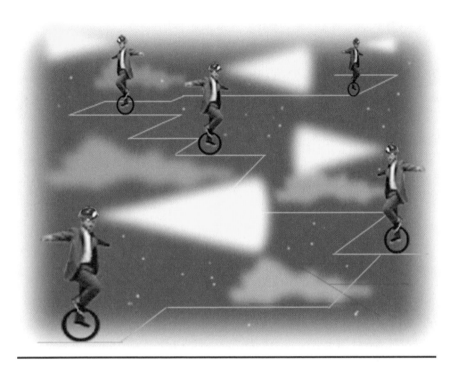

Chapter 6
Knowledge Mining – Focusing Less on How and More on Why

Data and information do not enable performance, but knowledge does. To understand knowledge management, we as CIOs need to have an understanding of knowledge. We need to understand relationships within the data, capture the patterns in the information, and extract principles of knowledge. We are in possession of knowledge when we feel we are acting based on intelligent data. Your networks will need to be responsible for collection, codification (organizing and representing knowledge before it is accessed by authorized users), and distribution of knowledge to your workforce in a timely manner. As CIOs we expect to optimize our business processes and remove knowledge barriers by adapting ways to encourage knowledge exchange among our resources. Network-based knowledge management tools can be critical to the success of business as we move toward the year 2020.

Indeed, many businesspeople would like to believe in the "black box," an intelligent machine that can help you navigate treacherous business environments, and a number of people have made a lot of money selling machines that promise to do this. Unfortunately, the black box doesn't exist. But the challenges your business faces every day *are* real. You need to make intelligent and quick decisions on many different fronts, based on huge amounts of data that any one person couldn't possibly organize. And while there isn't a black box that does it all, there are some increasingly sophisticated tools that offer a considerable amount of help.

A large telecommunications company, for example, handles hundreds of millions of calls each day, and accumulates data from each one: where the call originated, the time of day it was placed, where it was switched to, what local provider was used. A high-end data warehouse can provide the necessary storage and search capability.

Once the data is available, you can begin to apply techniques that mine all that information for helpful, and actionable, advice.

No More Time Lag

Data mining is a discipline that was born with the database. In the "old days," about thirty to forty years ago, data mining followed a very specific model. Data was collected in databases, and queries were run to retrieve account information, or sales records, or customer profiles. Different types of data weren't correlated; data mining was simply about storage and retrieval for purposes of archival or alert. A good data-mining application might help you understand when your plywood stocks were running low in your inventory, or what types of industrial equipment one customer preferred to buy.

Information mining was a step beyond data mining. Instead of drilling down to retrieve specific records, statisticians began correlating internal data against external data – information about the context in which the original data was generated. For example, stock-outs of plywood might be related to the seasonal occurrence of severe weather along the eastern seaboard. Perhaps people who are diagnosed with cancer live near industrial plants that produce a certain chemical. Patterns of data could be extracted by placing the data in context; the more data that was gathered and compared, the more patterns could be meaningfully extracted from it.

But even with this evolution, there was a significant time lag between the moment the data was stored and the moment conclusions about the data could be expressed. You could chalk this up to relatively elementary methods of statistical analysis or an overall lack of computing power – or both – but it meant that business decisions were at the mercy of an analytic time lag.

Advanced information mining entails a fundamental rearrangement of the information-mining model. Statistical analysis is moved upstream – meaning the data is analyzed *as it comes into the system,* before it's stored. Thanks to advances in processing power and data processing – advances that will only be extended by the large-scale distributed computing discussed in the last chapter – snapshots of the data can be taken while it's still in transit, allowing analysis to take place in real time. This means that businesspeople can act on information far more quickly and adjust their strategies within a day or two instead of within a month or more.

Fraud Fear

Consider this simple example. A young man decides to move cross-country. He has an outstanding credit card bill or two, but since he's moving to a new place, he guesses that he can skip out on the balance and start afresh with a new identity. After all, how will anyone be able to connect the two accounts?

Enter information mining. Habits are very hard to break, and even if people change their locale, or even their name, they still follow the same patterns in the services they use, the frequency, type, and volume of their credit card purchases, the websites they visit, and so on. In effect, they participate in the same communities of interest that they did before, even if their physical community has changed.

Powerful database systems, statistical models, and network matching algorithms – in combination with smart people applying smart models to address important business problems – can play a role in constructing very detailed portraits of service use. John Doe is probably going to make similar purchases and use similar services no matter where he lives. These portraits are so consistent, in fact, that our models can identify individuals with an amazing degree of accuracy – over 90% true, positive identifications.

But here's where upstream, real-time analysis is most beneficial. By moving the analysis forward in time, John Doe's service portrait can be detected as soon as he sets up a new account – no matter how long he waits to do it – and you can act on it immediately

Mix and Match

Information mining can mix and match the data you collect in myriad ways. If you have enough data, the possibilities are endless. For example, information mining can use RFID data (discussed in Chapter 3) to create intelligent inventory systems and supply lines. Instead of discovering losses when the truck arrives at the store, updated RFID tags can let you know if losses are occurring in a certain geographical area, or under the supervision of certain employees or partners.

Or consider the content explosion sparked, in large part, by the proliferation of broadband. Using data from previous purchases, Amazon. com can infer the preferences of its customers, providing them with lists of "recommended books." When all audio and video media are online, it will be as if the entire nation, if not the world, is hooked up to monitoring meters. Preferences will be defined with a much higher degree of subtlety than before.

Likewise, marketing can be targeted to consumers' preferences in a much more precise, rapid – and hopefully less annoying – way. Aside from interrupting their favorite shows, why do people find commercials so irritating? It's because 90% of the commercials they see aren't telling them about something they *want*. But "granular marketing" can index the media preferences of the viewer or listener against the profiles of others who enjoy or dislike similar content, and offer advertising tailored to their specific preferences. This strategy isn't new – it's already happening on the Web – but it is still in its infancy. Eventually, it will apply to all media as it migrates to IP.

Yet another advance will be combining the power of upstream information mining with customer care. For simplicity's sake, let's use VoIP (voice over Internet Protocol is discussed in Chapter 2) as an example. When a customer calls a service center, she hits tones on her telephone keypad in order to reach a specialist who can help with her specific complaint. Those tones route the call to the appropriate expert. Once a call is logged into a customer care center, VoIP allows you to "bundle" information to the call. So when the service call is logged into the company's database, the entire history of the customer's interaction with the answering tree becomes part of the record. If a frustrated customer calls repeatedly about the same problem and is always routed to the same place in the tree, upstream information mining will capture the touch-tones the customer has selected, and also note that the problem hasn't been resolved. Reports can then be generated to list all these frustrated customers, and customer service representatives can contact them *directly* to resolve the problem.

Or, if we regard customers with certain complaints as being an ad hoc community of interest, new service possibilities arise. A customer service representative can create a live conference call, invite all the users who are having the same problem or complaint, and define the issue far more quickly. (He also won't have to call so many people back.)

Implementing Information Mining

Upstream analysis is a powerful tool, but it isn't a solution that most companies will be able to develop themselves. On the other hand, using a vendor to supply your information-mining needs will also be a tricky process. Most "homegrown" upstream analysis and information-mining applications develop gradually within companies that have been using them as an essential competitive weapon for quite some time. Many financial services – pharmaceutical and retailing companies, for example – have developed useful applications. But the inner workings of these databases are generally kept under tight wraps. So a CIO seeking to implement a state-of-the-art information-mining system needs to develop a deep understanding of the type of analysis that will benefit his company before choosing an outside vendor. You need to know what your customers – your internal sales, marketing, product development, and customer service departments – need to be able to do. In choosing a vendor to work with, look for one with a significant track record. And beware of vaporware, which has plagued the knowledge-mining industry.

Of course, your work doesn't stop there. You'll need to consider what tools and capabilities you'll need to support the applications your internal customers envision. Are your networks robust enough to get the data to the data warehouse? Is the data warehouse sufficient to store the amount of data you need to operate with? Are your data compression schemes advanced enough to allow easy retrieval? How good is the data? Will it yield actionable strategies during analysis? What visualization tools do you have available to deliver and package the data? Finally, you need to ensure that your analytical tools are ready to move from "classical" data mining to upstream information mining. Your tools must be able to deal with large snapshots and cross-sections of a vast stream of data rather than one static database. In all likelihood you will have to rely on an outside source to provide most or all of these technologies as well. We need to introduce new units of measurements that we can relate to applications such as HDTV movie download, digital life-size video conferencing, and tracking object movements and their behaviors.

The table below shows the relationship between the file storage sizes that computers use. Binary calculations are based on units of 1,024, and decimal calculations are based on units of 1,000. It should be noted that decimal calculations are based on units that have been rounded off to the nearest 1,000 and therefore differ from the actual number of bytes used in binary calculations.

Name	Symbol	Binary	Decimal	Number of Bytes	Equal to
kilobyte	KB	2^{10}	10^{3}	1,024	1,024 bytes
megabyte	MB	2^{20}	10^{6}	1,048,576	1,024KB
gigabyte	GB	2^{30}	10^{9}	1,073,741,824	1,024MB
terabyte	TB	2^{40}	10^{12}	1,099,511,627,776	1,024GB
petabyte	PB	2^{50}	10^{15}	1,125,899,906, 842,624	1,024TB
exabyte	EB	2^{60}	10^{18}	1,152,921,504,606, 846,976	1,024PB
zettabyte	ZB	2^{70}	10^{21}	1,180,591,620,717, 411,303,424	1,024EB
yottabyte	YB	2^{80}	10^{24}	1,208,925,819,614, 629,174,706,176	1,024ZB

The Power of Knowledge Mining

Knowledge mining can be enormously powerful, and companies that deploy it will enjoy tremendous advantages over companies that don't. Consider how knowledge mining helped turn around one telecommunications industry giant. In the mid to late 1990s, this company's lead was eroding – a transformation was called for. The company needed to aspire to zero cycle time for customer orders and zero defects in services. To accomplish this it needed to automate as many internal transactions as possible, so that different systems across the company wouldn't unknowingly promise one type of service and deliver another, and so that human beings would not unwittingly introduce errors into these transactions.

Knowledge mining became the cornerstone of the transformation. Every company has procedures – some conscious, some not so conscious – that govern the way it does business. And with an enormously complex company such as this corporate giant, there are often so many processes and systems that it becomes almost impossible for one person to understand them all, let alone decide which procedures work and which don't. The divisions that existed at the time made monitoring all these procedures nearly impossible.

The company decided to approach the problem in a novel way. While computers can't *think* for us, they can process and store far more information than we can. So its computer systems were programmed to keep track of business processes, and told what the criteria for success was: the satisfaction of the customer's need. The systems kept track of the definitions of success and failure, and measured their own interactions against these definitions. Pattern-recognition algorithms were added that could recognize very minute changes in the company's processes – changes that would escape human detection. Successes could then be matched to specific processes. The systems monitored themselves, and it worked so well that salespeople and provisioning teams *trusted* them. The company's systems were designed so that they could mine *knowledge*.

Of course, knowledge mining isn't a simple plug-and-play solution. It took a lot of time and patience to work through the many challenges involved – synchronization issues among all the disparate data management systems, and building trust between the nontechnical staff and the machine learning systems, to mention just two.

Implications of Knowledge Mining

Knowledge mining isn't simply about managing customer service, collections, and other "subjective" tasks. Other industries face different challenges than those mentioned above, and they implement knowledge mining to streamline and improve physical processes instead of virtual ones. Oil industry giant British Petroleum used machine learning to control the crude oil and gasoline separation process, which is complicated by minute idiosyncrasies in storage and delivery mechanisms. A task that previously took one day or more was reduced to ten minutes. Printing companies use machine learning to eliminate imperfections in the printing process. Pharmaceutical companies leverage machine learning to determine drug interactions by modeling chemical structures in three dimensions – an activity nearly impossible for human modelers to do on their own.

In the future, this transformation of information into knowledge will dramatically change the way all information is networked. Distributed databases using intelligent search engines will be able to continually learn from the patterns of how businesses gather information and execute decisions. Nodes of the distributed network can then learn to relate the information gathered in one part of the network to information gathered elsewhere. Instead of separate pools of information, we'll create a collaborative knowledge network. And as time goes on, these knowledge networks will have incredible amounts of data at their disposal, available at faster and faster speeds – as we discussed in Chapters 3 and 4.

That data will include standard data, but also speech from VoIP systems, audio files, images, and video streams, all of which will be delivered over IP, and all of which will be indexed and searchable. Knowledge mining depends on having copious data and the processing power to manipulate it. Since both these resources are increasing enormously, we'll see a corresponding increase in the number and sophistication of knowledge-mining applications as well. Finally, since much of the data will be publicly available on the Internet, knowledge mining will also be performed by consumers to help them explore their interests and solve their problems.

Think about this example. Your company mines current and historical sales data, and discerns buyer habits and preferences. This creates actionable knowledge about how to fill the supply chain – what products, parts, or elements to purchase. But additional information from other areas of the converged network – such as weather, cultural trends, economic events, or demographic shifts – can be sifted automatically by your business systems, enhancing the accuracy of your original data-mining efforts. Thus the whole network works in concert to create better knowledge – and a new knowledge-driven way of doing business.

Vision: Supercomputing, Any User

No one will be left behind. Everyone will be transformed into a superuser, able to share access to supercomputers so powerful and rich in capabilities that relatively few will be needed and all will be shared.

Student, teleworker, city planner, teleconference participants, virtually anyone from around the world could well connect to the same supercomputer as the university research team, the civil engineer, and the agronomist – at the very same time, adding up to many thousands of simultaneous sessions running without latency.

Processing capacity will have doubled by 2014 to 128 bit array processes with Gigabit I/O.

The CPU will be obsolete. End users will simply access network-based computer clusters that effortlessly handle many users at once. Utility computing will be the basis for application-aware networks. On-demand services will take advantage of grid computing networked as a supercomputer.

NextGen computing could well achieve what the United Nations has not – true international collaboration and cooperation.

Collaboration of NextGen computers will encourage as well as enable collaboration among dispersed and disparate people, resulting in greater understanding and sharing in solving problems across boundaries.

The network is the key component in NextGen IT infrastructure.

Technologies Underlying NextGen Distributed Computing

The technologies that will collaborate in the realization of NextGen distributed computing include grid computing, Access Grid™, P2P, and adaptive computing.

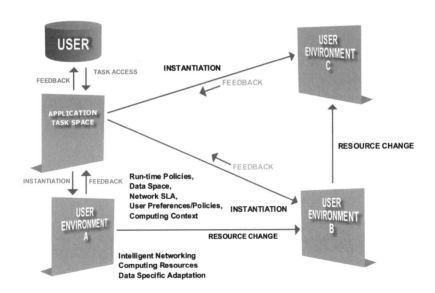

Grid Computing

Grid computing, the use of a computational grid, applies the resources of many computers in a network to a single problem at the same time – usually to a scientific or technical problem that requires a great number of computer processing cycles or access to large amounts of data. To accomplish this, software is divided and farmed out into pieces of a program to as many as several thousand computers.

Think of grid computing as distributed, large-scale cluster computing and as a form of network-distributed parallel processing. It is also known as wide-area distributed computing.

The Internet is used to build distributed computing and communications infrastructures. The emerging grid infrastructure enables the integrated, collaborative use of high-end computers, networks, databases, and scientific instruments owned and managed by multiple organizations.

Grid computing is network-centric and virtualizes geographically dispersed storage and computer resources. Grid functionality:

- Enables cross-organizational access and sharing of IT resources, including data, compute cycles, applications, and expertise over networks – the Internet and private intranets.

- Combines and integrates unparalleled computing power to solve problems that could not be resolved otherwise.

- Allows IT to be delivered as a utility, including network- delivered applications, e-commerce and B2B, hosting and bandwidth, storage utility services.

- Delivers quality of service (QoS) in security, availability, and reliability.

Grid computing is implemented by open protocols, services, and standards.

In the peer-to-peer (P2P) communications model, each party has the same capabilities, and either party can initiate a communication session. In some cases, peer-to-peer communications is implemented by giving each communication node both server and client capabilities. In recent usage, peer-to-peer has come to describe applications in which users can use the Internet to exchange files with each other directly or through a mediating server.

On the Internet, P2P is a type of transient Internet network that allows a group of computer users with the same networking program to connect with each other and directly access files from one another's hard drives. Napster and Gnutella are examples of this kind of peer-to-peer software. Corporations are looking at the advantages of using P2P as a way for employees to share files without the expense involved in maintaining a centralized server and as a way for businesses to exchange information with each other directly.

The user must first download and execute a peer-to-peer networking program. After launching the program, the user enters the IP address of another computer belonging to the network. Once the computer finds another network member online, it will connect to that user's connection.

Automating Collaboration

Once a process has proved successful, we can make it automatic. Since knowledge-mining systems are continually updated to refine and improve their own operations, they allow human resources to be freed for other endeavors, thereby reducing overall costs. Funds can then be dedicated to distributed-computing technologies that process and store larger amounts of data for our knowledge-mining technologies to exploit. More data means better decision-making, so that eventually our effort in extracting and acting upon knowledge from this system becomes minimal.

These automated processes "sit" on top of every technology we've discussed so far. So let's consider another example that illustrates how all these emerging technologies can work together. Say you're a commodities broker. IP-enabled sensors will provide you with real-time weather reports. The enormous data required by these sensors to monitor weather conditions will be transmitted by wireless broadband to vastly powerful distributed computers that collaborate on highly accurate weather-prediction models. Knowledge-mining software, having observed these patterns for some time, will compare the success or failure of a crop in any given season. If it rains in Kansas, the next day you will be informed – automatically – to buy futures. All these technologies are assembled in concert as a vast community of technological interest, which forms and disbands and reforms again, according to what we want or need it to do.

Try to imagine a world where the processes that have historically consumed most of our labor and effort – that have demanded our most intense collaborations – have been, in the main, automated. Labor and effort will never disappear, but these precious resources will be freed up through the power of computerized collaboration. Eventually, as we move toward 2020 and beyond, the application of knowledge mining will allow for the vast automation of many different processes – from financial decisions to military maneuvers; from the distribution of entertainment to the distribution of food. It will allow us to manage our environments with ever greater precision and accuracy. It will let us focus a little less on the how, and a little more on the why.

With so much at stake, system failure is not an option. In the next chapter we discuss the all-important questions and issues surrounding network security.

"Information security has been a challenge since day one, and no doubt it always will be. What we have to do now is move from reactive monitoring to predictive monitoring, to be able to eliminate threats closer to the source and catch them when they're further up the food chain."

— *Satish Mahajan,*
CIO and Vice President,
AAA Information Services

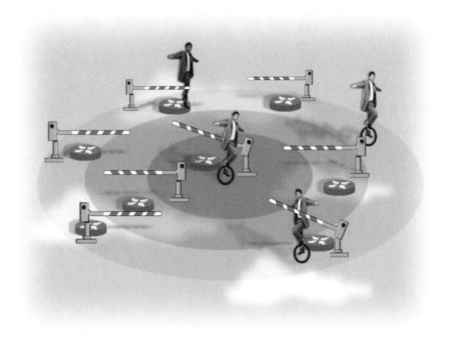

Chapter 7
Security – Guarding the Network

No CTO or CIO – or anyone else for that matter – would argue that network security is not essential. It is one of the few technologies embedded as part of every service that employees use. It takes many forms – physical (locks, bolts, vaults used to secure rooms, etc.), electronic (surveillance, sensors used to monitor areas), and personnel (training, employees used to operate these systems). And as threats to the network evolve, so do security technologies meant to combat them. The goal is to stay one step ahead of the attackers, and while there is never likely to be a perfect network security solution, there are techniques that can enhance the chances of your enterprise staying ahead of the attackers.

The scale of your network can be a great advantage in staying ahead of the game. A company with vast network traffic can use advanced tools and technology to ensure the integrity and privacy of its own network operations as well as some of its customers'. And as attacks advance and viruses morph, scale is likely to continue to be important in containing and controlling new threats, just as it was in August 2003 when the Nachi worm appeared.

The Nachi worm searched the Internet for systems that were vulnerable to an even nastier worm, MSBlaster, which had recently ravaged the Net. Once it identified a system as being vulnerable, Nachi patched the system to make it safe from Blaster. But the Nachi worm caused its own crisis. Nachi tested for Blaster-vulnerable systems by sending Internet control message protocol (ICMP) messages across the Net. These status messages, normally used to report on general network performance, propagated faster than many networks could handle them, and soon Nachi was flooding system after system. Corporate and government systems crashed.

Almost no one was prepared.

The Nachi attack and others like it are a reminder that a few lines of malignant code can jeopardize your entire network – paralyzing your services and your business. And if the challenges of securing the global network aren't met, the effects of those attacks will become far more dangerous than they are today. Indeed, there's no debate among the experts that the global network needs to be secure in order for it to reach its full potential. The challenge, of course, is how that can be done.

Security enforcement focuses on three key categories, known collectively as the three A's: authentication (Who are you?), access control (Are you allowed to do what you want to do?), and auditing (What did you do once you gained access?). What follows is a brief discussion of each of these important areas and how they are likely to change in the future.

Authentication

The first and most basic task of authentication is to secure an environment. Who is demanding entry? Should I let that person in? The simplest and most familiar authentication method has long been the individual password and user ID. But passwords and user IDs will soon be superseded by more sophisticated advances.

Technologies called biometrics – like the automatic fingerprint-recognition and retinal scans you see in James Bond movies – are becoming commonplace. The latest IBM ThinkPad˚ notebook computers, for example, have built-in fingerprint scanners to ensure that only you – or someone you give permission to – can use your computer. Future advances in sensor technology will soon make it possible to detect and identify individuals using other unique biological traits such as vein patterns, facial seismography, odor, and even direct identification of DNA.

Airlines, like Germany's Lufthansa, are developing tiered security policies that allow users to voluntarily submit to advanced biometric scans. Passengers who wish to make it through security checkpoints faster can purchase tickets imprinted with images of their thumbprints. The tickets can then be instantly checked against a scan of the passenger's thumb, authenticating them as the proper bearer of the ticket. Additional "real time" background checks can then be run from the security checkpoint itself, allowing local authorities to match the print against the records of various law enforcement databases. These procedures should make air travel far more convenient and security efforts far more precise.

Authentication also has to take place within the network, guaranteeing that remote workers or business partners can securely log in and access corporate applications over a public network infrastructure. Increasingly, however, instant collaborations between devices are creating authentication challenges for service providers and device designers. Because the devices are talking to each other without human supervision – automatic bank transfers, for instance – new methods of authentication oversight need to be applied.

This is going to be both more sophisticated technologically and simpler for the end user at the same time. As more intelligence is embedded in devices, and more devices leverage the advanced security provisions of IPv6, devices will be able to identify one another without reference to an outside authority like a security server. The main issue for most businesses is whether or not their service provider can handle this scale of transactions. Future improvements in authentication will need to be based on improvements in administration – meaning the speed, efficiency, and accuracy with which networks accomplish this vital task.

A carrier used to dealing with scale can often help reduce the complexity of authentication management. Knowledge mining is the key here – the ability of the technology to sort through various bits of information to make the crucial authentication decisions. This enables human administrators to manage increasingly automated authentication decisions at a very high level. And there is no room for error. Customers – like banks, brokerages, and others in the financial services industry – demand and expect 100% accuracy, no matter how large the scale of transactions.

Access Control

Once a system decides who someone is, it can enforce policies about what he or she should be allowed to do. Often the functions of authentication and access control are encoded together. Sensor technologies like RFID (discussed in Chapter 3) will be able to attach very specific authentication and access information to many different devices – from company ID cards to implanted medical information tags. As time goes on, authentication and access control functions will become more and more unified, so that one swipe or pass of the device can satisfy many different networks – from the security checkpoint at your job to your bank account.

By entering all of its employees into a database of record (DBOR) – a central repository for all user privileges and access capabilities – a company is able to keep track of whether an employee can access a certain asset in its system.

Ideally, the DBOR should be managed in real time. Real-time management means that security breaches can be isolated and corrected as soon as they are identified. There are two prerequisites for adapting a DBOR-like solution. First, you must have a data warehouse that can hold all the access information. Second, you must have intelligent network monitors for building an accurate inventory of security requests and actions on a global scale.

As systems for managing access-control grow more powerful, incredible progress is also being made in cryptography. Cryptography has progressed from the simple alphabet ciphers of antiquity to nearly uncrackable computer encryption. By 2020 computer processors will be capable of conducting as many as a trillion encryptions per second. That's a decidedly mixed blessing, for it will benefit equally not only those trying to encrypt information but those attempting to crack the codes as well. The good news is that powerful encryption will be available for lower-end devices. And since most garden-variety hackers do not have access to superpowered processing speeds, this means that most elements of the network will be well protected.

One certain beneficiary of these advances is likely to be the area of digital rights management (DRM). The coming encryption advances will make the comprehensive control of content and delivery not only possible, but likely. Stamping technologies will be able to validate the source, destination, and date and time when a file was created, and how long it can be "owned" by any receiver. Comprehensive DRM will be a boon to every business that needs secure communications – especially the entertainment and news industries.

Yet no matter how secure DRM becomes, there are two security holes that technology can never close – human error and human duplicity. Cryptographic algorithms that are theoretically unbreakable exist now, but management of security infrastructure involves people and processes, both of which are subject to corruption. No access or authentication technology innovation can replace the judicious selection and monitoring of those who have access to secure assets. And that's where the third aspect of security comes into play: auditing.

Auditing

The first step in moving toward increased virtual collaboration is to ensure that the networks that *do* the collaborating are secure. This can be accomplished by the constant auditing and monitoring of traffic for suspicious or malicious activity. A service provider can program knowledge-mining techniques into its network to analyze and assess the security dynamics of network traffic. These large-scale, highly precise threat assessments will allow it to automatically update the security policy for its routers, pipes, and servers. Security measures will propagate faster than security threats, making its network strong and reliable.

But what about *direct* threats to customers themselves? Using knowledge-mining technologies, a good protection service can warn you that there's a huge wave of email-propagated spam circling the Net *before* it reaches your machines. Similarly, if a "denial of service" attack is flooding a part of your network, the protection service will see it, automatically reroute the traffic, and send it through a scrubber where good traffic is separated from the offending flood. The offending traffic will be analyzed and, if necessary, shared with law enforcement authorities. Your servers will continue running as if the attack never happened.

In both cases, the provider's technical capabilities and rapid response time *leverage* the scale of their network. As we move toward 2020, the types of protection customers can expect will become faster and more powerful, because service providers will have more and more data to feed their knowledge-mining processes. Potential threats will be detected much earlier, and response time will become close to instantaneous. The key is that knowledge-mining techniques enable *flexible* security. A rigid or fixed security system is a perfect target for hackers, while a more flexible system presents a much greater challenge.

Auditing the Edge

Every service provider has a vested interest in keeping its network running smoothly. But the future of security lies at the edge of the network as well as inside the network itself. The edge is the largest threat to network security, because it's the place where foreign elements can most easily enter and wreak havoc. Trojans of every stripe – viruses, worms, "malware" – can be introduced by consumers and employees over myriad devices. Threats and attacks are becoming increasingly sophisticated. Indeed, they evolve so quickly that it takes enormous training and experience just to identify where they originate.

Unfortunately, every individual who owns a PC is in effect a systems administrator, no matter how little technical training they may have. While they're responsible for auditing all the activity on their own machines, most users barely know they have been charged with this task. An entire industry – the managed security service provider, or MSSP, industry – has emerged to the aid the individual "system administrator." Personal firewalls and security services were developed for the home user and the small business network starting in the mid-nineties. But left to their own devices – literally and metaphorically – end users generally make poor choices when it comes to security, frequently falling prey to the malicious and criminally minded.

If this weren't worrisome enough, end users are frequently the victims of extremely poor engineering decisions and the astounding complexity of current software. The software they use is generally poorly designed, with little or no thought given to the security implications of the code. Buggy software is responsible for the vast majority of security problems facing the telecommunications network.

Truly comprehensive training and education for the next generation of software engineers would be one major step toward addressing security concerns. Ed Amoroso, a security expert, likens the present discipline of software engineering to the state of medicine during the Civil War. The typical field surgeon's tools might have been limited to a bottle of whiskey for dulling pain and a couple of very scary knives. The software engineers of 2020 will no doubt look back on today's engineering practices as being similarly crude.

But recommendations on how to change software design aren't enough. We need to take additional steps. We need to rethink network design, too.

Preemptive Auditing

Klingons, for anybody who is not familiar with *Star Trek*, are the warlike race that had a nasty habit of attacking their adversaries in "cloaked" spaceships – craft that were invisible to even twenty-fourth-century technology. It is possible to adopt the cloaking idea for purely defensive maneuvers necessary to protect a network, allowing customers to leverage statistical information regarding current threats and attacks from the network. Security risks identified in the network trigger updates in the edge device's security policies.

Think of this as a preemptive intelligent auditing technology. If an attack or virus issues from one machine or system in the network, the rest of the devices will be inoculated against the attack almost as soon as it happens. In this way the network becomes invisible to attackers, because the main avenues for the attacks – the edge devices – refuse to admit or pass along the dangerous traffic.

This type of security – extension of the network security to the edge devices – may be the only way to keep up with the proliferation of devices and sensors expected by 2020. There is no way to manually "patch" edge devices when they number in the trillions. To manage devices at that scale, proactive network management techniques are required.

Preemptive auditing is just a first step in a new type of network design that will stop hackers and criminals in their tracks. The philosophy behind cloaking needs to be expanded to ensure a trustworthy environment for collaboration. Perimeter security controls, like MSSP software, need to become a thing of the past. The network itself should automatically provide security policies and procedures to the local laptop or PDA. Antivirus protections and patches to buggy software need to be downloaded to the edge before a threat is widespread, preventing the spread of attacks. As a result, all networks – and end users – that rely on this type of infrastructure will share in all these up-to-the-minute security policies.

By bringing intelligent auditing to the edge of the network, we begin to take the first steps toward a truly secure internal network. Adding this task to the overall network management equation creates fewer interfaces and less opportunity for error. Still, some businesspeople – not to mention consumers – might be nervous allowing an outside company to auditing *all* its traffic. But these "Big Brother" concerns are largely unwarranted. Auditing traffic for security purposes is much different than snooping through the content of the traffic. It takes place at such a high level that it poses little or no privacy risk.

Auditing Between Networks

But what about threats that come from other networks – not from your network or your service provider's?

Here's a hypothetical dilemma. You're the sheriff of a small town. You get a call one night from the sheriff from the next town over, and he gives you some disturbing news. A raucous motorcycle gang, intent on mischief, is heading into your jurisdiction. "They're speeding past my police station right now," he says. "Just wanted to let you know."

"Well, why don't you stop them before they get here?" you ask, puzzled and alarmed.

"Consider yourself lucky," he drawls. "According to my service level agreement, I didn't even have to call you!"

Because the network infrastructure is shared among several large companies, and leased or used by thousands more, there's a concern that suspicious or malicious activity that's generated from within one company can come as a surprise and create problems for another. In other words, how do you ensure that your network isn't blindsided by the security lapses or mismanagement of another company? How can well-managed networks communicate possible threats to one another?

Wouldn't it be better to know that an attack is coming? To know what provisions others have taken – or *not* taken? To gain a wider view of current global network traffic and threats? To share auditing information across networks? Of course. We need to develop a simple, open, flexible, and on-demand infrastructure to share security information and policies. If we do this, we can have a truly secure global network.

A model to accomplish true global network security already exists.

Networks of top-level providers communicate over IP traffic routes using a border gateway protocol (BGP). BGP is a set of rules that governs the interaction of our infrastructures and intelligently routes traffic among our networks. Because of BGP, our individual IP networks interoperate smoothly. And as we discussed in Chapter 1, individual networks are exponentially more powerful when you allow them to share information and users.

To create truly secure interoperating services, we need to build a security border gateway protocol (SBGP). There's nothing like this now, but the organic growth of local solutions indicates that it's beginning to develop under our noses. SBGP will hold networks accountable to rules that define *secure* collaboration. An SBGP infrastructure would be both flexible and scalable, so that special security policies could be deployed between any two customers' or partners' networks. You and your partners, for instance, could leverage the power of each other's networks by allowing a network provider to ensure secure collaboration.

If implemented, these collaborative security efforts among large-scale network and service providers will create much smarter, predictive, and preventative security policies by 2020. Additionally, the increasing popularity of open-source software engineering – and the transparency and community cooperation that accompany it – will help eliminate software bugs as a serious security risk. Inventing better ways to control the complexity of the systems being created for computers today will also help.

It's quite possible that we are experiencing the historic peak of security incidents against networks worldwide, and that these incidents will slowly fade into minor nuisances as the next decade unfolds. This will free up CIOs to focus on enabling services, rather than managing security. And if that is indeed the case, the payoff could be huge. The safer networks are, the greater the likelihood that networks will join together. And, as we've seen, convergence creates value. Every additional member of the network is another n in the 2^n equation that defines the power of the community networks. The potential for growth is enormous.

If networks become even safer, CIOs will be able to turn their collective attention to other just as challenging but perhaps more productive concerns. One particularly exciting area with great potential is the development of smart environments, a subject we explore in depth in the next chapter.

The Power of Legislation and Ethics

We will continuously refine procedural legislation to complement the security infrastructures embedded in every device and core product. There will be international treaties that give Internet governance jurisdiction over anyone, globally, for as long as they can show evidence that proves "cause for an action."

By the year 2020, we will have radically changed the traditional approach to dealing with deceptive software. The new rule of law will call for applications to follow certain internationally mandated guidelines to provide a self-defense application free from the possibility of infection. Lawmakers will have a greater need for scientists and technologies to lead them in drafting new legislation to would put severe restrictions on the use of so-called traditional spyware.

Arguably, Congress and world lawmakers would have agreed on the Internet and multimedia access policies that restrict the use of uncertified applications, components, or devices on public networks. Combating spyware will not be as complicated as in the years 2004–2010. By 2020 we will have made significant strides regarding who can launch software in the public domain. The analogy of needing a driver's license to navigate on highways and streets also will apply to being able to launch applications in the Internet domain.

Ethics and collective actions will play a key role in dealing with defectors. The basis for better behavior is similar to what we have learned from eBay, where doing business requires maintaining established credit. This new era of balancing technology, law, and ethics will continue because users will no longer be able to hide behind their IP and Mac addresses, or use proxy servers. New technologies such as self-defense application designs (networking, storage, computing), sensory solutions, RFID, and tagging will complement new ways of making the application users and owners visible for traceability.

The explosion of intelligent multimedia networks and object trace tracking solutions will create peer pressure to follow Internet and regulatory policies.

With the success of more secured networks, the traditional role of law firms to provide services to society at large will change. Law firms will turn into online service providers, and judges will be much younger in age, with a broad background in Internet law.

FUTURE PREDICTION

Smart environments, equipped with sensors and actuators, respond to local or remote automated or manual controls, and this, in effect, helps them become part of a larger knowledge system. By the year 2020, smart environments will have tremendous impact on our applications, networks, and computing resources.

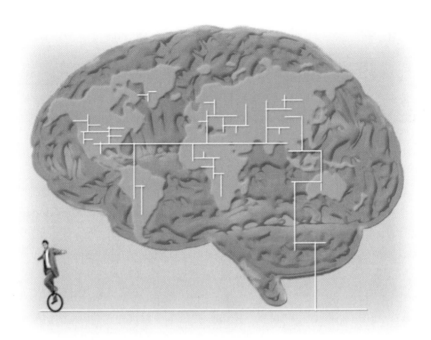

Chapter 8
The Smart Environment – Using Technology to Self-Regulate

In Chapter 4 we discussed the ongoing work in the last mile of broadband access and how telecommunications companies, cable companies, and even some municipalities are working to deliver high-speed, extreme broadband (XB) to homes and businesses. Now envision the year 2020, when IPv6 (discussed in Chapter 2) will create enough possible addresses to provide *one million IP addresses per square millimeter of the earth's surface* – from a small patch of concrete sidewalk to a bobbing square on the ocean's surface. Sensors attached to IP addresses will be able to report information about these "environments" – no matter how small they may be – and large-scale distributed computing and knowledge mining capabilities will use this information to help executives make sound business decisions. The battle then will be over the last millimeter – the last square millimeter, to be precise – of connectivity. This infinitesimally calibrated information will help us to manage our business more effectively than our competitors; more important, it will allow us to *collaborate* – on a grand scale. At the same time, it will present significant new challenges and opportunities for CIOs.

To a certain extent we're already familiar with "smart" environments. Consider the heavily automated, robotized automobile assembly line pioneered by Henry Ford back in 1913, almost a hundred years ago. It's an environment designed from the ground up to turn huge chunks of metal into cars. These days advanced automation techniques – including intelligent software and closed feedback loops, which are very fast and use adaptive software – create the product and monitor the success or failure of different components of the system. Or consider the RFID supply-line or inventory-control system (discussed in Chapter 3). These systems are, in effect, large-scale smart environments. They are designed to report on their condition, from the warehouse to the delivery truck to the stock room. The information they provide allows top-down intelligent management of the resources. Both examples were designed to be intelligent from the start. They illustrate what we're after with the smart environment – intelligent monitoring and manipulation of resources.

Truly smart environments, however, use technology to self-regulate.

Our attempts to create a truly smart environment – an environment with intelligence "baked-in," so to speak – actually began closer to home. Long before Bill Gates built his celebrated automated home, long before *The Jetsons* or *2001, A Space Odyssey*, people dreamed of creating futuristic home and office environments that take care of themselves – performing menial tasks, monitoring safety and security, and entertaining us in multimedia suites. And some limited progress was made in this direction. Technologies like X10, for instance, were created. X10, which became available in the 1980s, was an appliance control system that directed the functioning of lights and appliances through signals sent across electrical currents in the home.

But these early efforts didn't create smart environments; they simply produced a parallel network that ran across and through an existing network in the home. That's because in their present incarnation, buildings exist as a nexus of several arbitrarily related networks – the power grid, the telephone network, cable lines, and water and gas pipes. Without a network-unifying protocol, buildings can't become truly self-regulating environments. This is already happening with telephone and cable networks. (Some visionaries see IP being delivered directly over the power grid, creating further network convergence and simplicity.)

The smart environment of 2020 will use IP to tie all resources together intelligently. Appliances, machines, computers, devices of every stripe will communicate with and be managed by the environment. But before we focus on how IP manages smart environments, let's talk about how the smart environment of the future will have built-in intelligence from the ground up.

Baking It In

Building construction itself is undergoing a revolution. On the simplest level, building materials like wireless-friendly building insulation are becoming more popular because they allow wireless signals to operate without obstruction. But in the future, the materials themselves will be able, through wireless sensors and responsive engineering, to report on their status.

Consider this example. There's a suspension bridge in China called the Dong Ting Lake Bridge. It looks like a normal suspension bridge, but when you take a closer look at it in heavy winds, you'll see something that *must* be an optical illusion. Every one of the suspension cables is swaying violently, except for one – which is absolutely still. This particular cable has been retrofitted to test the viability of smart building materials. It is housed inside casings that carry a special fluid. Inside the fluid is a suspension of extremely small magnets. Individually, these magnets are only a few molecules long. When the wind blows against the bridge, sensors send different electrical pulses through the fluid solution, reflecting the direction and force of the blast. The magnets in the solution line up in different formations depending on the electrical pulse, causing the casings to tighten or loosen. The cable still moves, but it moves in response to the conditions of its environment, creating a more stable structure.

As nanotechnology – the engineering of extremely small structures – improves and becomes more economically viable for consumer applications, more and more building materials will exhibit this kind of environmental responsiveness. This will lead to huge leaps in safety for newly constructed homes and communities. (No doubt there will also be enormous profits to be made from retrofitting "dumb" homes into smart structures.)

In addition to providing significant structural benefits for buildings, such as reducing damage from tropical storms and earthquakes, smart materials will create a revolution in energy conservation. Smart materials – paint, for instance – will detect temperature levels throughout the surfaces of buildings. Not only will they be able to report the atmospheric conditions of the building more efficiently, smart materials could actually report on areas of the building that are leaking heat or losing their cool, thereby saving the owner a lot of money on his gas bill – not to mention conserving the nation's energy costs.

The Intelligent Office

At the same time that building materials are changing, intelligent offices are evolving from existing converging networks. The drive toward extreme broadband – especially in its wireless forms – is setting the stage for tomorrow's smart environments. Workers can move around and communicate anywhere inside a wireless office environment, and their devices are increasingly tied to one another in comprehensive service offerings that may be unique to the facility. Cell phones, desktops,

PDAs, and other devices are all wired together seamlessly to encourage productivity and efficiency.

However, much like the X-10 systems described earlier, the wireless-enabled office of today is still just a new type of network laid on top of an office location. As these networks converge toward one another, we will come closer and closer to the flexibility of service that enables true smart environments. But there's still one essential ingredient missing, and that's the ability of the system to self-monitor and self-regulate.

There's a term we use in telecommunications called *point of presence* – POP, for short. A POP is the point at which one local environment – a city or a neighborhood – accesses the rest of the telecommunications network. Internet service providers (ISPs) can have hundreds of POPs throughout the country, depending on the size of the company's network.

The POP manages all the traffic for that local region and provides the gateway for services delivered over IP. It manages quality of service issues, such as the reliability of connections, as well as class of service issues, such as routing traffic depending on the urgency and importance of the particular traffic. In the intelligent office, the individual local network operations center, or LNOC, will become, to coin a phrase, a "NanoPOP" – a point of presence for all the services that the intelligent office offers to its users, both via the Internet and internally.

The LNOC will provide several basic functions for the future business environment. It will *monitor* performance, usage, and energy demand for appliances and devices. It can also monitor the health of the infrastructure and all its connected systems – LANs, phone lines, electrical wiring, walls, roofs, and plumbing. Finally, the LNOC can monitor people while they are in the office, tracking their movements, behavior patterns, schedules, and use of machines and devices.

The LNOC can take the data collected from all these applications, devices, sensors, and cameras and *analyze* it to determine patterns and identify anomalies in usage, security breaches, and opportunities for more efficient functioning. Alerts can be generated and actions performed so that intelligent office systems operate more efficiently. Analysis and control will ultimately be determined by the office manager's preferences, and usage policies determined by the CIO. These human rules will be combined with intelligent suggestions from the LNOC.

The LNOC also offers another important advantage. It will be the gateway from the office to the larger IP network. Any IP service will be available in the office, through all its connected devices. As more and more intelligence is programmed into the devices that are already commonly used, the LNOC will evolve in order to "knit" these smart devices together.

The Subject Is Objects

Beyond managing and integrating ever smarter technological devices, the intelligent office of the future will manage and track as many different types of objects as human managers can name and label. But not just "objects" as nontechnical types think of them. Rather, the term *object* has a specific technological meaning that it would be helpful to review.

Object technology is a programming philosophy that organizes data into virtual objects. Computer languages that are "object oriented" support object-oriented programming. Objects have certain basic states, just as real objects do. The object "book," for instance, will have certain manipulable states (page number, subject, paper type, author, etc.). Like real objects, some of these states are fixed (the date a book was published), while others are malleable (the price of the book).

Additionally, programmers, applications, or users can perform actions (called "methods") on these properties to manipulate them. They can request information as to the condition of the object itself. (How old is the book? How many pages does it have?) They can also request that they perform actions on other objects (the object "reader" can read the text of the object "book"). Objects can specify the extent to which other objects and users can interact with them. (Is the object "reader" mature enough to read the book?) Objects are organized hierarchically by property. Finally, objects can "belong" to other objects. In other words, we can associate a group of objects with one or a group of other objects.

What does this have to do with smart environments? The objects that programmers now use are entirely virtual, a way of creating services and applications. But intelligent offices will allow a CIO and technology team to manipulate real objects in similar ways. Ways that mean significant changes in how we do business.

Think of your offices, or even a larger facility like a warehouse. There are thousands of objects throughout any of these environments – products, workers, industrial machines, sensors that monitor utilities and energy use. With the use of sensor and tag technologies like the ones we discussed in Chapter 3, every one of these objects can be labeled and monitored from the central LNOC. And because of RFID technologies, these labeled objects will be able to report their current status to the LNOC. Was the laptop that's being removed from the building signed out? Is the guest who just entered the high-security area authorized to be there? Where is the CEO's PDA?

Every one of these objects "belongs" to the office LNOC, and that's what makes the LNOC the final ingredient in the smart environment recipe. The intelligent office LNOC manages its assets in a *self-interested* way. It's not merely a combination of discrete networks; it's not about useful services offered over converging networks. It's about the intelligent management of an environment as an entity.

Consider an intelligent department store. The store "owns" the objects that come within its perimeters. When customers check for product availability over their PDA or from their desktop at home, they are querying the LNOC of that particular department store, which monitors availability in real time, by detecting tags on all of the products. Simultaneously, the LNOC communicates with the inventory systems at the home office to let the consumer know when a sold-out product will be restocked. The LNOC is letting the home office know about particular responses to a recent marketing campaign. It's also keeping track of the suspicious movements of certain product tags on the third floor – and alerting nearby security guards. It's notified maintenance that there's a broken window on the basement level, which is wasting energy by overworking the air-conditioning system. At every step, the LNOC is taking care of itself, following the rules and criteria set up by the company's IT policies.

The smart environment is the fruition of every technology discussed in the book so far. It relies on IP addresses connected to sensors and tags that label and describe every object worth tracking. Wireless extreme broadband permeates the environment, ensuring that all the objects' current states can be discovered and reported. Distributed computing provides the power to handle all this information elegantly and in concert with the home office above and the consumer below. Finally, knowledge mining and machine learning strategies regulate and refine LNOC behaviors and strategies to make the whole facility perform at optimum efficiency.

No one is "doing" intelligent offices or businesses like this yet. You can't buy an LNOC product and set up a smart environment. But the pieces are all there, and CIOs at the most forward-looking companies are slowly beginning to knit them together.

Intelligence Extended

We've already talked about how network service providers help customers design intelligence into their supply lines and inventory systems. These companies will also be in a unique position to provide management of smart environments once those environments come online.

We saw how individual smart environments "own" the objects within their perimeters. But things become more interesting when we consider that every LNOC is an object in and of itself, that can be "owned" by other environments. The retail store we described above is just one of many objects owned by a larger enterprise, which of course has its own LNOC. And once we see that these individual environments – no matter how large – are objects for even wider-scale monitoring, analysis, and control, we can envision the business- (and world-) changing implications of smart environments – and the next great frontier for CIOs

Imagine an LNOC that "owns" your truck fleet. Each truck already has a degree of intelligence; several computers in the engine regulate performance and emissions. The traditional dashboard gages won't disappear, but they'll be augmented by a series of monitors that can tell the manager of your fleet which vehicles need repair, or what the gas mileage is for the entire fleet. The fleet LNOC can also track the precise location of each truck and reroute lost drivers or send out repair trucks automatically in the case of breakdowns.

If every vehicle has an onboard LNOC, smart roadways also become possible. RFID tags have already revolutionized toll collection through programs like E-ZPass and FasTrak. But smart cars can do more than pass quickly through tollbooths. With a minimum of investment, wireless routers can be deployed along the highway. They can report the position and velocity of passing vehicles so that traffic management becomes intelligent. Accidents and roadway blockages can be monitored and dealt with proactively. The nation's roadways become smart environments that "own" all the vehicles traveling on them. Those same routers will enable the smart car to deliver many different types of entertainment to drivers and passengers, from Internet radio stations to video and gaming entertainment (for passengers, of course).

And beyond all that, governments and international organizations will also be able to monitor large-scale natural events. An early warning over IP could have mitigated the impact of the devastating December 2004 tsunami in Indonesia that claimed an estimated 230,000 lives. As it happened, international barriers and incompatible equipment kept one country from reporting the magnitude of the wave to the next. Environments that are the nexus of national and natural security concerns (seismic fault lines, national borders), large-scale business systems (supply lines), and preexisting network environments (the power grid, roadways, and telecommunications networks) will likely be "owned" by large monitoring systems belonging to governments, enterprises, or consortia of both.

It's possible that by 2020 all our environments – from the consumer's home office to the nation as a whole – will be able to communicate and collaborate with each other, and with us. As time goes on, these environments will be able to share physical resources with each other, much as grid computer technologies share virtual resources like processing power. Think of how this will change energy usage, or shared supply lines, or large-scale transportation. The shape of the world will be much different in 2020, because we'll be able to manipulate our environments in very powerful ways. And that, in turn, will allow us to take the next step toward convergence, discussed in the next chapter.

FUTURE PREDICTION

The distinction will be less about separate wired and wireless technologies and applications, and more about service portability between various networks – seamless service mobility. The network of 2020 will leverage both smart devices and network intelligence to delivery services in this seamless fashion.

Chapter 9
Convergence – A New Universe of Services

T he best networks don't just meet our needs. They anticipate them. They prevent difficulties from occurring. And they proactively provide new services. By altering the notion of what networks can do as a whole, we're coming closer to an environment that is truly predictive, preventative, and proactive.

The process began by extending security to edge devices, as discussed in Chapter 7. This first step offered the basic services that all networks must guarantee: trust and reliability. The next step: networks will evolve even further by becoming sensitive to our physical and virtual environments – the smart environments we spoke about in Chapter 8. At this point, networks will be *predictive*. They will constantly gather data about our physical environments and help automate decisions and actions in the real world. These new smart environments will make

117

our physical world smaller, more interactive, more helpful, and more manageable.

But, paradoxically, as the physical world becomes "smaller," the virtual world of information grows. And the more information we have at our disposal, the more *proactive* network services can be. *Any* user can be the center of a converging universe of services. Indeed, the network will be built around the user.

Converging Architecture

Let's return to one of the concepts addressed in Chapter 2: how IP is able to deliver any telecommunications service. The simple term that sums up the convergence of telecom services through IP is XoIP. XoIP stands for X over IP, where X stands for any service whatsoever. VoIP is an XoIP service. So is streaming audio. So is IPTV. As are the huge number of applications gathered under the term *Web services*. And we've seen throughout this book how one service after another is slowly being transformed by the open, flexible, and robust structure of the IP network.

Service providers of 2020 have many complex challenges ahead of them. The software engineers who will make smart environments a reality and the networking companies that integrate services within smart environments will need more than just active imaginations. They'll need a network architecture that makes interconnectivity possible.

The structures that a large telecommunications provider builds for reliable and secure networking become the hallmark of what it does. But every time it adds a new service, it's faced with the challenge of how to integrate that service into its network. In the past, such a company might offer a new service, but be forced to roll out an implementation tailored specifically for the individual telecommunications systems in each region. Often it would have to build a new service for each of its customers. This type of implementation is called *vertical engineering*. It means erecting new technological structures, from the software down to the wire, every time you want to deploy a service. And it's a vestige of the past.

Now network providers strive to offer all their services to all their customers, regardless of idiosyncrasies of network or device. It's crucial to be able to handle many different devices and to intelligently manage the myriad ways they communicate. The XoIP infrastructure makes this possible.

The Power of Layers

The XoIP infrastructure divides telecommunications into four separate layers.

- The *device layer* includes traditional phones, wireless phones, computers, PDAs, etc. *Any* device that can network.

- The second layer contains *access technologies* – all the myriad methods that devices use to communicate with each other and our network – copper wires, wireless, cable, Ethernet, etc.

- The third layer is the *network connectivity layer*, which is where IP comes into play. This layer provides a basic set of capabilities *independent* of the device or access method the customer is using. It recognizes users – authenticates them, provides access control, and connects one device to another; but most importantly, it processes requests to the final layer.

- The fourth *service layer* contains software-driven service intelligence that uses the IP traffic of the network connectivity layer to process service media. The service layer might store and save your conversations, for instance, or convert your conversations into text, or serve you custom television broadcasts based on your past preferences.

By keeping these layers separate – but with open, standards-based, published application programming interfaces (APIs), so that anyone can connect between them – service providers can make them agnostic, meaning that they don't need to know what the other layers are doing, just what the other layers want. The application layer communicates commands to resources in the lower layers, which are structured on-the-fly to deliver the service requested. The centralized command in the application gathers a community of technological interest – from the sensors, pipes and ports, all the way up to the machine-learning and knowledge-mining capabilities that tailor and structure services. And as more resources are shared among companies across distributed computing systems, more combinations of resources can be knit together into unique service offerings.

This XoIP infrastructure innovation targets the borderline areas between the layers. In the past, every device was dependent on a certain access technology, which in turn allowed certain services to be built for that device – but only for that device. Handing off communications between these separate silos – moving services available on the traditional phone network to wireless phones, for instance – was a daunting challenge. But by allowing the different layers to communicate with each other seamlessly and agnostically, and controlling the gathered resources at the application level, providers can offer the widest variety of services to the widest number of customers and users. Services that combine the capabilities of different devices become possible. The openness of the architecture allows for the building of powerful and flexible services that can be offered universally to all customers, and to open the innovation engine to third parties to multiply the numbers of new services offered well beyond what one company could do alone.

You don't have to run a vast network to create these services yourself. Everyone, from equipment providers to software companies, is leveraging the power of IP to create or support innovative services. Equipment providers are creating PBX machines that are IP-integrated and provide

VoIP service. Software companies like Skype are creating proprietary, peer-to-peer IM-like VoIP applications that are just simple pieces of software available for download and distribution. Of course, it's helpful to leverage the expertise of a company with network mastery, scale, depth, and many partners it can leverage to help you build your services when you're developing or deploying your own XoIP services. After all, if your network isn't good, how good will your services be?

We are witnessing a fundamental change in the telecommunications industry, from vertically integrated service offerings to "horizontal" offerings. Instead of a few companies creating tailored solutions, different companies, playing at different layers in the XoIP architecture, are providing different components in the service suite.

Extending XoIP

As our discussion implies, XoIP wouldn't work without its openness to and support of standard IP-based protocols. These protocols make converged network services possible. Take SIP (session initiated protocol), for instance. In a traditional phone network, a caller sends a signal over two separate networks. The first – the control network called SS7 – routes the call. The actual call itself – the audio signal that carries the voice – is sent over a separate but parallel service network. When you set up the signal over the control network, you connect the phones, and then tear down the control signal that routed the call to free the circuits to route other calls. The service network connection remains open until one of the participants hangs up their phone. This control/ service separation leads to enormously reliable service. With SIP we can use the same model to create a parallel Internet standard for VoIP that mimics this strength and reliability. This same standard enables other XoIP services – especially entertainment services that rely on audio and video, or messaging services.

Extensible markup language, or XML, will become the lingua franca for describing and exchanging data among XoIP services. XML is a tagging system for data, allowing communication between services and devices that might not normally be able to talk to one another. XML is so flexible and easy to use that developers are using it to create a variety of languages tailored to specific industries and their needs. Voice XML is the key to many of the voice-oriented features that will become part of XoIP.

The XoIP infrastructure is being developed in close relationship with the industry supported IMS (IP Multimedia Subsystem) architecture. IMS will be the springboard for seamless delivery of multimedia streams across mobile and wired devices. And IMS helps enable VoIP service and audio-video services like video conferencing with the reliability and high quality expected by today's consumer.

All these IP-extending protocols enable services like VoIP and IPTV – services that straddle many different access devices. They both depend on easy access between devices and different access technologies. In this way, XoIP allows voice and/or video service to be delivered to any compatible device that a subscriber uses, as long as they sign in and request service.

At Your Disposal – Services Anywhere

But the integration of smart environments – like the smart home, or the smart car or office explored in the last chapter – into the XoIP infrastructure produces an interesting result: the people who use these environments can be freed from them.

In the past, wireline telecommunications networks identified a "user" by a telephone number, which was associated with a certain location: a house, an office building, etc. When you called a number, you called a fixed location. Anyone who picked up the phone at a certain location was assumed to be the user by both the network and the person making the call. And if the same person picked up a phone in a different location – a friend's house, the office, or an airport pay phone – then that person was, with few exceptions, assumed to be a different user. The limit of traditional telecom is that it offers services to locations, not users. Similarly, users had to access different networks (cable for TV, phones for voice communication, etc.) for different services. All this will change with the arrival of XoIP.

On the most basic level – and we're already seeing this change – we'll experience the continuing erosion of the notion of "local" and "long distance" as separate services. VoIP has already begun this process. Users with a VoIP telephone adapter (TA), the "box" that connects the user's phone to the network, can plug it in wherever they find a high-speed connection, and the "phone" number will be available there – maybe thousands of miles away from "home." Additionally, users will be able to dictate their service preferences to the network. Intelligent XoIP services can accept preferences about the time certain communications may be received, or the days that all communication should be blocked.

Besides, the XoIP infrastructure allows the service to adjust and adapt to the access technologies the user has at his or her disposal. Let's say you record a video message to a business partner who is on the road, and his or her wireless phone doesn't support video. The message can be converted by the service layer from audio-video format into an audio message and delivered to his wireless phone. Or it can be translated into plain text for delivery via email or IM.

Likewise, you can imagine a service that seamlessly hands off communications between devices, depending on the location of the users and the devices they have at their disposal. If your wireless phone loses reception as you enter your office, the call can be seamlessly transferred to your office phone. If your office phone is tied up, or you only have access to your laptop, voice-recognition software will translate your friend's voice into text; speech-synthesis software will translate your typed text into audible speech for your caller.

Finally, suppose that your workers didn't have to carry around valuable laptops and telephone adaptors, but wherever they went they could plug into any available device and have their business environment appear, just as if they were sitting in front of their desktop. Right now, on a GSM phone, you can remove the SIM card from your cell phone and plug it into the chassis of another phone, and for all intents and purposes, the new chassis *is* your cell phone. The intelligence is swappable. But consider a device agnostic card, similar to the cell phone SIM card but carrying just enough intelligence to get your employee to your network and to leverage every service you can offer through that device. As devices become more intelligent, and distributed computing systems become more prevalent, all your employee would have to do is stick in their card, anywhere they want, into any device, and retrieve *exactly* the same resources and applications they have on their PC.

The entire spectrum of business applications, news, and entertainment will be delivered via IP to users across a multiplicity of devices across a multiplicity of environments. Television, music, films, newspapers, blogs – each can be adapted for a user's active device, on the fly. Only the limits of the device – along with the services that a particular user has subscribed to – will dictate the way it's delivered. Essentially, the user's concept of what the network is, and what the network does, will change drastically. Subscribers will expect services to be delivered to them regardless of location, and regardless of the specific device they're using. The user will be surrounded by network services, built around their current location, access, and need.

Virtual Services

The freedom that XoIP offers doesn't stop with the mobility of the services themselves. Services will become increasingly virtual.

A lot of people watch two televisions at the same time. They're busy people, who need *lots* of information to manage their businesses. They might tune in to a news channel on one set and a stock market report on the other. And somehow they manage to get enough information from both sources with minimum interference. It's quite a skill. But there is a limit to how much information even people like this can process.

Scientists estimate that the human sensorium – all the nerves and nerve endings in the body, from almost nerveless internal organs to the hypersensitive eyes, ears, and nose – have a total bandwidth of 2 Gbps. But because broadband speeds will eventually far exceed this 2-Gbps limit, it becomes possible to transmit the entire range of information that any one person's senses could take in at any given time, even assuming optimal human reception. We may be able to transmit virtual reality, made up of sights and sounds, perhaps eventually smells, tastes, and textures as well.

It is now possible to create data visualization systems that allow very large, very complex sets of data to be mapped so that a user can visually "surf" through data. Instead of having to imagine relationships between data shown in conventional graphs and charts, the user can see patterns at a very high level of complexity – hundreds of millions of records per day over years – and then drill down to individual records, all within a graphical interface. All the evolving patterns of a company's network traffic, for instance, can be seen ebbing and flowing in real time, and users can drill down to any level of data, no matter how complex.

As holographic projection technologies improve, users will be able to "move" seemingly within landscapes of data, turning information into environments to be entered and explored. Researchers, for instance, have created a "data cave" for the three-dimensional visual representation of data. They use it to predict complex chemical reactions. They can literally watch computers arrange and rearrange the chemical particles from *inside* the molecular structure. Instead of sifting through reams of data, scientists can recognize knowledge – complex patterns of data – that they might have otherwise missed.

Over the past decade, early versions of technologies such as Telemersion and virtual reality have emerged in a number of labs. Telemersion allows different individuals in highly distributed locations – e.g., designers of structures or industrial equipment – scattered around the globe stand in accurate 3-D renderings of their work, and see the same environments, at the same time, as they will appear when completed.

On the TV show *Star Trek,* one of the featured high-tech innovations is a holodeck, a virtual environment that replicates all the sensory data of a real environment. The holodeck may not be with us by 2020, but certain characteristics of it are already here. For example, the recent Titan probe detected methane levels in the atmosphere of Jupiter's largest moon. It was a technological extension – across half the solar system – of the human nose.

XoIP infrastructure is a first step toward making virtual services widely available. The ubiquity of virtual services requires a high level of interconnectivity and network intelligence, a hallmark of our business. Consider the possibilities for the field of marketing. Virtual representations of physical products – clothes, for instance – could allow users not only to see the color of the fabric they're buying, but feel its texture as well. A network will become an environment in which we can meet, socialize, learn, and create. It's an environment that can respond to the desires and needs of the community. It's the beginning of the converged world.

Business and Social Impacts

Indeed, the converged world emerging from a foundation in traditional telecommunications will change our daily lives in ways we can only begin to imagine right now. But already there is one central feature that can be perceived now, even before the details come into full focus. The business community, as well as every other community of interest, is being freed, slowly, from the constraints of time and place. Of course, people will always be attached to their individual locales – their homes, their neighborhoods, their towns and cities. We're bound to them by family ties, personal connections, and social and cultural history, among other things. But when it comes to communications, we will soon be largely free of temporal and geographic constraints. We will be able to do business, socialize, entertain, interact, and collaborate with one another in the way we like, from wherever we are, whenever we need to.

Consider using networking technologies to work from home. The physical location of the employee in the service economy is slowly taking a backseat to other considerations – expertise, competency, and the amount the worker is willing to accept as salary. But employers' newfound freedom in utilizing far-flung workers also extends to the employee. As time passes, employees will be liberated from the constraints of the workplace as well – the need to commute or live in areas in which their services are in demand. There will be other benefits. Fewer commuters may lead to a cleaner environment – less fumes and less pollution. Less travel time will mean more time for work, which could increase productivity, one of the key measures of economic success.

Finally, the convergence of these unlimited service possibilities expands our immediate environment to include a much wider universe. The number of possible interactions for any one person – in business, entertainment, or education – will become effectively limitless. Already, members of the generation that grew up with the Web, cell phones, IM, blogs, email, and SMS keep in constant touch with much larger communities than any previous generation imagined possible. Communities themselves will become reordered around shared concerns, capabilities, and interests.

It's conceivable that these XoIP-enabled interactions could have a disruptive effect on individuals' ability to manage their lives and environments. Just as human beings can manage only so much information, evidence suggests that they can manage only so many relationships. Some scientists believe that the human mind is engineered to manage, at the most, 150 to 200 relationships. Even the IP network, which significantly extends our ability to forge communities, follows certain geographic patterns based around virtual localities. It turns out that these localities are very similar to patterns in the physical world, like traffic patterns between large cities. But instead of building up around physical resources, the information superhighway wraps itself around shared interests – business endeavors, scientific projects, commerce, hobbies, education, and the like.

Convergence and the CIO

The primary concern of the CIO in this emerging environment is the integrity of information. Looking over their entire enterprise, he or she needs be certain there are no errors or losses of any of the data and information being served up to the users in the network. As the flow of information increases, this in itself is a big job, but as we move toward 2020 the responsibilities of the CIO will only expand further. CIOs will increasingly become key players in making their companies competitive. They will need to create applications and services that optimize resources, both human and technological, to save time and increase productivity. Thus the CIO is destined to become not just an information manager but, perhaps even more important, an information strategist as well.

Designing applications that your customers – whether fellow employees or external constituents – want becomes an even more vital part of the CIO's job. How many windows are opened before the service pays off? Is the service tailored only to one type of device? How inconvenient are the security provisions? Can you make the service easier to use without lowering security standards? Are you backing up their devices for them, no matter where they are using them? Are you creating automatic collaborative environments? Does your customer automatically get to the person who can solve their problems? Is your infrastructure smart? Self-healing? Self-improving? Are you setting up your applications so the user's experience is beyond positive? Are your networks proactive? Are your network and information infrastructures ready for the next groundbreaking service, even though you don't yet know what it will be?

The bottom line is that users should feel like they're part of the network. Surrounded by the network. Served by the network. No matter where they are, or what device they use. They are expecting this type of service more and more every day. And if you can prepare your company to offer advanced services like this now, you'll get an enormous jump on the future and earn a real competitive advantage.

How will this transform networking? Future networks aren't just about exchanging data. They will exchange large amounts of command and control data. The network of 2020 is going to be built around an increasing number of objects signaling across the network: signaling action, signaling requests to other objects.

Every technology we've discussed contributes to or supports this architecture. IPv6 creates the additional address space for all these nodes (and more). Universal XB service will enable the delivery of data-rich services. Grid computing and other distributed-computing technologies offer a robust collaboration infrastructure built to manage large-scale scientific applications. Knowledge mining and machine learning create the intelligence required to offer truly customized services. XoIP, with its roots in the bedrock of IP, will spread and flower into unlimited service possibilities, distributed throughout all our networks. We're already witnessing the early stages of convergence among these new and emerging technologies. But, it's just the beginning of the level of convergence that will be possible in the future.

Chapter 10
A Day in the Life

Time Tunnel

As a child, one of my favorite television shows was *Time Tunnel*. It was a *Lost in Space*–style drama about a team of scientists hopelessly trapped in a malfunctioning time machine. It had all the hallmarks of 1960s sci-fi TV: questionable acting, garish sets, and, for that era at least, *really cool* special effects.

But I didn't care about production values. I was fascinated by the idea. Every week the scientists would wind up in some exotic time and place – on a spaceship bound for Mars, for example, or in the middle of the Trojan war, or on the decks of the Titanic. (Luckily for us, the tunnel had a tendency to drop the scientists in to the most dramatic times and places.)

And all I could think about, as I watched, week after week, was this: Could I predict the future? Could I look around me, at the past, at the mundane present, and understand where it was all going? Could I help us get there faster? What would happen to me along the way?

I haven't seen the future – but it's been my business to make informed estimates, predictions, and along the way, to help invent the future. And I believe that, unlike the science fiction heroes of my youth, we don't need to design special technology to transport us to the future.

We only have to look at the technology we have now, and see where it's leading us.

———————————————•◆•———————————————

Robin's off to work. She has to commute today, which is rare, but there's a good reason for it.

"Shower: A hundred and five degrees," she says, as she stretches and gets up out of bed. She hears the shower come on strong in the bathroom. Robin is an architect who specializes in building safe structures. Today, she's being summoned to a construction site about a hundred miles south of her home in Berkeley, California. There was a small seismic shock a few days ago, during the first days of construction, and the contractors want to know if conditions are safe to proceed with the construction. Since delays cost the contractor a lot of money, Robin will travel to the site. Unlike most business events, verifying building integrity is something that can not be done virtually – soon maybe.

At the construction site, Robin supervises the technicians who are spraying down the foundation of the new office complex with smart dust sensors. As they settle over the site, Robin will use the data from the sensors to check the foundation for any weaknesses that may have developed in the concrete.

While she waits for the results to download into her laptop, she receives a call on her personal communication assistant (PCA) from her father.

Some things never change, Richard thinks as he sits on his porch in Queens, New York. *Doctors always keep you waiting.* Richard has just sent in his latest body-report to the SUNY virtual medical lab upstate.

Then again, he thinks, *some things do change for the better.*

A few passes of his home bodychem reader – like the medical scanners he used to see on *Star Trek* when he was a kid – replaces all of the needles and blood work he would have undergone twenty years ago, all in the comfort of his home. Tiny sensors in his bloodstream do all the work, and the bodychem reader securely uploads a precise biochemical profile to the lab in an instant. All those people, waiting in a room to see the doctor, he remembers from the website pictures, just like the old days. *Another thing that's better,* he thinks, *my porch beats a waiting room any day. And I've got a much better choice of reading material.* He flips through a menu on his PCA and glances at headlines from his favorite major world newspapers and magazines, looking for something to pique his interest, when the lab sends back the results over his PCA in a short text message: *You're fine.*

Richard only uses voice on his PCA; he's never gotten used to the holograph projector, much to the chagrin of his grandchildren. He "dials" his daughter by saying her name; the network reaches her on her job site.

Anonymous results from Richard's body-report are compiled, along with millions of others, into a massive distributed database at the Food and Drug Administration. Abina, a medical researcher in Austin, Texas, uses a new holographic database navigator to "walk" through the medical history of American seniors. As a grad student, she used to have to correlate hundreds of separate studies on different illnesses and conditions; today, she's able to stand in a virtual immersion room and examine data flowing in three dimensions over a map of North

America. *Why,* she wonders, *didn't they have this in grad school?* Abina was trained as a practitioner, and she was always better at seeing patterns intuitively than compiling abstract figures and charts. Something catches her eye. "Clear," she says to the air, and the flowing holograph disappears.

"Remap, please." She laughs – she's amazed at how polite she is to the computer, but it's hard not to think of it as a colleague sometimes.

"Map one: reports of carcinoma, 1970 to present. Map against: incidence of environmental exposure to …"

The lights dance before her as she adds pattern on top of pattern; her work is so engrossing that she almost forgets her lunch meeting with her cousin, Kwaku. Luckily, her PCA remembers, and buzzes quietly on her arm.

Kwaku is lost. It's his first trip to Austin, his first trip to the states, and he never learned English back in Ghana – he was too busy studying French. But right now, his French isn't helping him.

He knows he's supposed to meet Abina at the Hospital Drive entrance to Waterloo Park, but he's positive, now, that the last half hour of pleasant meandering he indulged in has got him irretrievably lost. The map of Austin on his PCA isn't helping him, because the park isn't fully mapped like the rest of the city is – it's just an undifferentiated green patch in the middle of roadway grids.

Then he sees it, on the path a few feet away – a thin, black obelisk with a flat video screen. *They have these in Accra,* he thinks. *The tourists are always standing around, talking to them.*

He steps up to the video screen. "Maahá," he says. The screen comes to life. A map appears with a friendly face woman's face inset in the corner. "Yemu!" she replies. Kwaku follows her directions, and exits the park on the corner where he is supposed to meet his cousin.

Abina is late, so Kwaku takes a moment to initiate a video chat with his co-worker Michel in Metz. While he's been enjoying his vacation, Kwaku knows that the home office has a big virtual-texture manufacturing contract up for grabs, spanning suppliers and manufacturers from Europe, Asia, and Africa – IP networking has really flattened the world of business. Michel is in charge of putting the bid, all of it, together. He pings Michel over his PCA and sees that he's busy, in the middle of a meeting – but Michel has left the videoconference open for observation by his employers and co-workers. Kwaku is absorbed in the details. Minutes later, Kwaku meets Abina at the right spot.

"You found it!" She says, smiling. Kwaku nods, signs out of the conference, and gives his cousin a hug.

"Of course!" he says.

Michel watches the flatscreen intently. His entire team is assembled – Eileen is videoconferencing in from the virtual meeting room in the chip factory outside Dublin; Raman is on video at the call center in New Delhi; Ed, as usual, is waiting to catch a flight – this time at Kotoka airport in Accra. He's using the virtual meeting room there. Xuan is driving to local headquarters in Taipei, so he's only coming in over voice. All of the presentations are available for everyone to see, and the audio is ultrahigh quality. It is like being there, except for the twenty-four-hour hour flight. And, of course, there's James, who took some time off to go to the beach while he was in an Indian coastal province. Luckily for him, his PCA networked with other devices across the beach. *Other business people taking an afternoon swim,* Michel wonders? – and connected with the base station on the local wireless tower.

Michel gives a quick rundown of the latest numbers. Virtual texture screens have become very popular – the technology allows virtual conference rooms and other flatscreen devices to mimic the textures of actual fabrics, causing a revolution in textile marketing. The team seems to take a collective gulp when they hear the quotas, but Eileen and

Xuan assure the rest that the parts can be manufactured and shipped in time.

James, looking sunburned and contrite, offers his latest production figures over a spreadsheet that instantly downloads to all of the participants. He can make it happen, he says, but only if he gets off the beach and back to the virtual meeting room at his hotel. He's going to have to push his suppliers, and for that, at least, he needs to appear "in person" – virtually, of course – since some of the suppliers are a few thousand miles away. He signs out, and while the conference wraps up, Michel turns off the meeting recorder. The entire exchange has been recorded and saved, digitally, and a link to a replay – including all of the downloaded backup materials – will be sent to his design team instantly. He looks at the file size of the replay – not bad, only 10 GB. It should only take a minute.

Masatoshi is thrilled. Until a year ago he was retired, and as much as he enjoyed spending time with his family, it just wasn't right for him. *I need a challenge*, he thought. He was financially comfortable, but getting a little bored.

Fayed, a young designer from Seattle, "ran" into Masatoshi at a virtual lecture he gave on industrial designs about a year and a half ago. He claimed to be a big fan of Masatoshi's design work, and talked endlessly about how he had been influenced by him as a young design student. He spoke so passionately, in fact, that when Fayed approached him with a proposition for a business partnership a few months later, Masatoshi was torn. How could he spend time with his family while building a whole new business?

Maybe it's my age, Masatoshi thinks, reviewing the replay Michel just sent him at his home office in Kyoto. *But I still associate businesses with office complexes.* But Fayed had him convinced within just a few days. The young designer had sent him a complete business plan, a corporate presence, all of the trappings of a top-notch firm, even though, at the beginning, it would be just the two of them. *That will change*, thought Masatoshi. *We'll attract more talent. But who needs an office anymore?*

Fayed pings him on his PCA, and Masatoshi transfers him over to the video screen. "I've got the screen frame designs finished," he says, smiling enthusiastically at his mentor. "Do you want me to send you the holograph images now, or would you rather I send them to the 3-D proto-printer?" Masatoshi knows the answer Fayed wants to hear – he loves playing with the new three-dimensional proto-printer they purchased, which turns digital designs into actual prototype plastic models.

"Send it over the printer," Masatoshi says. "I've got a very important meeting in a few minutes and I need to use the immersion room. Thank you, Fayed, for the design . . . we'll need it sooner than we thought." He sends his young partner the link to Michel's meeting playback. *And thanks for making me feel a little younger, too,* he thinks to himself.

Masatoshi's oldest daughter, Akiko, is the only one of his children that he can't visit – she's studying cello in Buenos Aires with a master teacher, Elena, who insists that her students learn from her in person. "There is an element to art that cannot be communicated by a machine," she tells Akiko whenever she complains about missing Japan. But Elena's the best teacher in the world, and Akiko knows that it's worth it.

However, today she's going to try to prove Elena wrong. She's reserved the local university's virtual immersion room for a special performance. She sees her father on video chat every other night or so, and they talk, and review archival performances by the greats of the past, and current performers as well – they subscribe to a media network of classical musicians and music enthusiasts who create custom playlists, swap and exchange their own recordings, and review recent performances for the whole community. Every now and then she plays for her father, or sends him a high-quality file of one of her compositions, but today she wants to play for him in person.

Her father is already seated in the virtual concert hall when she arrives and starts to set up her chair, stand, and music. While they chat aimlessly about the local gossip and news from home, she notices that some more of her family members have joined them – her mother and younger brother are there to watch, and listen. Akiko gets a little nervous, but when she finally settles down to play, it's like there's no distance between her and her family at all.

When Akiko's private virtual concert is over and her mother and father step out for a walk in the city, Akiko's little brother, Natsuo, stays behind in the immersion room. He has friends he hasn't seen in a while – a group of five friends he met last summer during an international conference for scientifically gifted high-school students in New York City. He had walked the streets of New York virtually for years before he met his friends – sometimes strolling through the city with empty streets, sometimes standing in the middle of Times Square watching the traffic fly by at double speed. His father's media immersion room is often his favorite place to be, and when he is inside it, New York is where he visits.

Now the virtual landscape of the Big Apple feels lonely without his group of friends, the ones he explored the *real* city with. There's Kwame, from Baltimore, Edie, from Birmingham, and Sandra and Luis, siblings from Madrid. They meet once a month, virtually, to catch up, goof around, share new music, or watch movies together. They gossip and brag about their accomplishments. Each of them has an exciting project or two to discuss; tonight, it's Kwame's turn to brag. He's just won an internship on a revolutionary spaceship design project for NASA; there's an orientation meeting today and he has to leave his friends early.

When Kwame arrives at the converted warehouse on the outskirts of Baltimore, he's disappointed by how mundane the exterior looks – one of endless stretches of old industrial buildings on the fringes of the city.

He's a smart kid, and he's been disappointed before. Disappointed by academic "challenges" that he could master without much effort at all.

But once he's inside, his worries melt away. In front of him, surrounded by weathered bricks and iron girders, built out of nothing but light alone, is a spaceship.

Numerous engineers and scientists walk around the ghostly image. Some of them even walk right through it, suggesting changes to operators who adjust the design through a small console at one end of the building. As new contributions and adjustments are added, the image shifts and shimmers in response.

Where's the computer? Kwame wonders to himself. *What's generating the image? What's managing the design?* And then he sees it – an enormous data pipe running straight out of the wall, into the console, and then branching out from there across the infrastructure of the building.

Phil, a chief engineer on NASA's distributed aerospace design project, is tired. He's managing a project that's being worked on, simultaneously, in six different locations across the United States; the nation's best engineers are collaborating with him on an experiment that is the first of its kind. Besides the massive technical challenges, there's a constant battle for funds, and now, in the middle of an otherwise stressful but exciting night, he's summoned to be an expert witness at a meeting of a budget committee in Congress.

Naturally, the warehouse facility is equipped with a virtual meeting room; he plugs in a portable government-issue biometric scanner that registers his identity through fingerprint and retinal scans. The ID verification is uploaded to the Congress's security server; his face and title appear on a special monitor in the hearing room. *Now that I've used technology to prove who I am,* he thinks, *I'll have to spend the next two hours defending it from budget cuts.*

The congressional testimony is starting to bore Robin a little. She's a science and technology junkie – her business depends on it – but she's worked all day, and the committee seems to be covering the same ground again and again. "Jazz," Robin says. The testimony ends, and suddenly a fast-paced Miles Davis number fills the car. She's always amazed at how well the network radio subscription service she uses has learned her taste in music. *I haven't heard this one in a long time,* she thinks, *but it's a little too jumpy for me tonight.* "Miles Davis, *Kind of Blue*, track four." The music pauses, and changes to a slow, stately shuffle.

Robin is driving on an open stretch of road, heading back home. For the most part, the traffic is a breeze. There was an accident on the highway on the way back from the construction site, but an alert was issued to the navigation system in her car, which plotted an alternate route for her. She'll be home in a half hour or so, but she hasn't gone for a drive for a while, and she's enjoying it. She speaks aloud to the car again.

"Home system," she says. She hears a tone, signaling the command handover to her smart environment application. "Arrival time, two hours." She knows her house is expecting her soon; it's better to think ahead and save a little on the electrical bill. "Car," she continues. "Restaurants near San Jose, California. Italian, please. Somewhere nice but not too expensive. Surprise me." It's been a long day. She deserves it.

The car responds with audio list of five restaurants, and offers to program the quickest routes to each into the car's navigation system. She's about to pick one, and then she changes her mind. "Turn off navigation, please." The small screen with the highway map goes dark.

I'll surprise myself, she thinks, taking the first exit toward the coast she sees. *Sometimes it's more fun to find things on your own.*

The virtual world network will offer us freedom – the freedom to do business, to socialize, to communicate. In short, to interact free of many of the constraints we still feel in 2005.

But the science fiction fantasies of the twentieth century certainly predicted many things that never came to pass. Think about 2001 and the human colonization of the moon, for instance. It's hard to predict what technology will actually deliver.

The type of life that I've just outlined is one possibility; I think that many of the applications and services I've discussed throughout this book are likely, if not certain. But there are certainly different visions that are equally appealing and interesting. We are, after all, limited only by the boundaries of our imaginations, and no two extrapolations from the present will be the same.

But I do believe that the technologies we've discussed – that will shape our future – provide one crucial service above all else: they are flexible enough to allow us to communicate in ways limited only by our imaginations.

We have the tools to build many possible futures. It's up to us to use them wisely.

"It won't be long before video communications takes off in a big way. The idea of waving good night to the kids three thousand miles away is not so far-fetched anymore."

— *Nick Price,*
CIO and CTO,
Mandarin Oriental Hotel Group

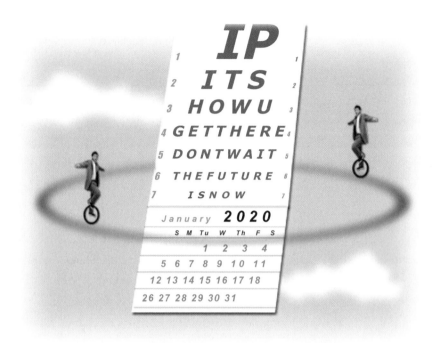

Chapter 11
Conclusion

Now that we've gone on this tour of the future together, it's obvious that I'm passionate about technology and its possibilities. I see life in 2020 as very positive overall.

But I'm also a realist: I know there are a number of barriers and challenges waiting for us along the way.

When we started this journey I compared it to a space flight; now that we've reached the end I think it's a metaphor that was well chosen. Hurling something the size of a rocket toward a distant, enormous planet requires a great deal of precision and power. And while navigational errors late in the game can be corrected with small adjustments, even miniscule mistakes made before we launch can make us land in a far less appealing world than the one I just showed you.

This book outlines the technological journey that we as a global community began forty years ago, and that has been accelerating at dazzling speed ever since. So far we've dealt with the technologies them-selves – the ones we've developed so far, and the ones that are fast approaching. Now it's time to acknowledge that with those advances come challenges – challenges for which we have to plan, challenges that can affect the ride we're taking as well as the world we will create. If we don't plan for and meet these challenges, we may not get there at all.

Applying the technology to deliver the 2020 services that customers demand will be the easy part – and only half the challenge. Also to be addressed will be the legalistic and moral challenges in the virtual society. While everyone will be an end user, their agendas will differ as people and institutions grapple with the responsibilities that come with all the new tools that enhance life, but also risk misuse and require new thinking.

2020 Vision: Cyber Civil Rights Movement

A new civil rights movement will develop. While the first one unfolded in the United States during the 1950s and 1960s to secure equal rights and protection under the law, the coming cyber civil rights movement will be global and virtual in seeking to establish equal Internet access as well as to define and protect cyber rights in the virtual society of the post-9/11 world.

The Department of Homeland Security, in its role of making America secure and protecting against future terrorist attacks, is bringing the challenges into sharp focus.

There will be contention ahead, as we face the seemingly conflicting demands for equal and full Internet access to data on the one hand, and security and privacy on the other. The debate will no doubt rage for years.

Cooperation will not be spontaneous or fluid. Collaborators initially will often seem like opponents. These will include technology companies, standards forums like the World Wide Web Consortium (W3C), end users led by enterprise companies, assorted interest groups often focused on a particular service or category, governments and regulatory agencies, lawyers and groups like the American Civil Liberties Union, the courts, and finally the individual consumers, who may or may not feel they are represented by the other groups.

Intellectual Property (Trademarks, Copyright, Domain Names)

With the advent of the Internet, the legwork needed to research and write an honors thesis or a front-page story accelerated to top speed as information from around the world became available in seconds.

Whether intentionally or through inadvertence, plagiarism and copyright infringement also accelerated and are unlikely to slow down by 2020, as more and more material becomes immediately available 24/7.

Problems in recent years with the unauthorized downloading of music and videos are a glimpse of the difficulties ahead in policing the infringement of intellectual property: trademarks, copyrights, and domain names.

The explosion of data and instant access ignited by 2020 technologies and services will also increase users' potential exposure to fraud, especially in online ordering where personal information is exchanged and financial transactions completed.

"The Internet offers a global marketplace for consumers and businesses. But crooks also recognize the potentials of cyberspace. The same scams that have been conducted by mail and phone can now be found on the World Wide Web and in e-mail, and new cyberscams are emerging," warns the National Consumers League.

Censorship and Filtering

The virtual society is all about freedom, mobility, and unfettered access to the Internet and its links to information. Unclear in the 2020 vision is the role, extent, and implementation of censorship.

Filters now exist that enable parents to block their children's access to material they deem inappropriate. Businesses today routinely block workers' access to sites not work related, such as computer game sites, sports links, and, obviously, porn sites.

Filtering technology and its resulting services will become the increasing focus of solution providers responding to the need of end users to protect themselves from intrusion, and material they stipulate they do not want. Filtering will also help to organize, control, and aggregate the information flood to make it manageable.

Yet even as civil libertarians press for privacy protection, they will also fight any efforts that seek to prevent adult access to material others may deem inappropriate, including pornography.

The technology to filter or completely censor is already developed. What has yet to be determined and what will be the subject of a protracted and heated debate is censorship itself. The questions are difficult.

W3C suggests there can be Internet controls without censorship through the use of Platform for Internet Content Selection (PICS) technology for flexible blocking. PICS, a metadata system, puts the control capability with the user rather than the sender. In this way, it's thought that recipient-centered controls will protect against the possibility of sweeping censorship imposed from without, by the government or other authority.

While PICS and other filtering programs can expect wide adoption in the United States and elsewhere, there will certainly be repressive countries where PICS would be seen as a threat. The government would seek to control the Internet, which would be viewed as a challenge to centralized authority, as it is in China.

Taxation

Currently, Internet access is not taxed in the United States, although Congress, always looking for new taxes to levy, has considered the idea. Congress has already passed the Internet Tax Freedom Act, which bans state taxation of Internet access. There is debate under way on whether or not to extend, modify, or revoke the online tax ban.

Proponents of the Tax Freedom Act want to extend and expand it, arguing that the tax ban is needed for the Internet to achieve its projected growth. Any imposition of taxes will slow the realization of wireless Internet ubiquity. However, those who want to repeal the act argue that it is costing billions in lost tax revenue to states and municipalities.

Additionally, critics argue that the online tax ban gives an unfair advantage to e-retailers, driving customers to the Internet while penalizing traditional shop owners who are forced to collect sales tax.

An additional attraction of online retail for both the buyer and seller is that neither is bound to a local market. The world is the marketplace, providing global choices for the buyer and potential customers around the world for the retailer.

Complicating the issue is the fact that transactions are increasingly transnational, involving not simply one state or even one nation's tax code, but the tax codes of many nations.

When Americans now return home from vacation or business overseas, the U.S. Customs Service collects duty on the imports. There is no online Customs Service – yet.

The Futurist magazine forecasts that major nations will be collecting Internet taxes by 2014. There's just too much revenue to be gained from online sales for it not to be collected.

But any initial attempts to collect taxes will be cumbersome and inadequate. International treaties are required and a consistent tax code must be developed.

Security and Privacy

The right to privacy, imbedded in the U.S. Constitution, is a cherished privilege. Protecting privacy – and the security of digital data – will perhaps be the greatest challenge confronting end users, network providers, data providers, governments, and police agencies.

What will propel the maintenance of privacy and security into the top ranks of the challenges ahead is the very openness of the emerging network and the power, tools, and freedoms the network delivers.

Additionally, post-9/11 reality requires heightened government surveillance of users, websites, and user groups – including terrorists – and the data flowing across open network. The controversial USA Patriot Act gives coordinated and heightened powers to America's security agencies, which are closely monitoring Internet traffic for terrorist "chatter."

Balancing individuals' right to privacy and the security of data against overall security and free access will require applied technology as well as the goodwill and collaboration of all concerned.

Additionally, there must be new behavioral and legal ground rules. InfraGard, an FBI-led task force, brings together the federal government, various law enforcement agencies, network providers and other business representatives, plus consumer groups to examine these issues.

Enhanced encryption – to thwart terrorists as well as cyber criminals – will be essential to protect privacy and secure data and the Internet. Enhancing encryption and offerings will be a nonstop process. The stakes could not be higher. The bad guys are determined, smart, and sure to test the system.

In addition to applied technology, the response to privacy and security challenges must also include tight export controls and enforcement to guard against 2020 tools falling into the wrong hands.

In its role as the protector of America and its people, the Department of Homeland Security, with its sweeping powers and surveillance tools, has raised concerns from civil libertarians, among others, that individual privacy is threatened.

Networking Industry's Role

Industry needs to take the lead in securing systems – technologically and operationally.

The essential first step is the collaborative establishment and enforcement of standards through appropriate forums such as the World Wide Web Consortium and the FBI-lead InfraGard. The latter is a public and private alliance of the FBI, state and local law enforcement, and the private sector to share information and conduct analysis to combat terrorism and cyber crime, including invasion of privacy and security breaches.

The very same technological breakthroughs that will usher in virtual society with its benefits and threats also have the capacity to protect 2020 end users.

Government's Role

September 11, 2001, changed America and the world forever. There's no going back to the way things were.

America remains the world's most open society. Yet there have been and will be adjustments and compromises to be made to secure the homeland and combat terrorism.

Government will set the rules, which creates concerns that in the post-9/11 era too much surveillance power and control will rest with the state and not the individual.

Congress will create new committees and will legislate hundreds of new laws; laws that will need to be regularly amended in order to keep up with rapid technological change and the flood of new tools and services, with their concomitant vulnerabilities and potential for misuse.

Expect a steady barrage of lawsuits, filed by the American Civil Liberties Union and others, battling to protect privacy and also fighting for no restrictions of access. Lawsuits will be put at the top of the docket and will be fast-tracked to the Supreme Court to establish legal boundaries, much as the industry is rapidly developing its own standards.

Heightened government power is inevitable in the wake of September 11. International treaties among the community of nations must be established to protect privacy, while ensuring freedom of access.

Since the Internet knows no boundaries, law enforcement agencies must collaborate across nations. Uncooperative nations and terrorist regimes must quickly be identified and monitored, isolated, and economically pressured to come into compliance to reap the benefits enjoyed by the community of nations.

Balancing the two goals of protecting privacy and protecting society will not be easy. Inevitably there will be swings back and forth – excesses demanding immediate correction and measures to prevent reoccurrences.

Individual Responsibilities

Society's basic, long-established principles of good citizenship remain sound and apply fully to good cyber citizenship.

Just as neighbors now must get involved to keep their communities strong, so too Internet users in 2020 must get involved and work together to protect each other and the virtual society they inhabit. Otherwise, that society will become more dangerous, users and their data less secure, and their privacy lost.

As much as possible, end users must be able to decide for themselves what protection they need and what restrictions they will permit.

While one person, or one household, may feel powerless – collectively they represent a powerful force.

New interest groups, standards forums, and cyber civil rights leaders will emerge to work with and against existing groups. Institutions and government agencies, operating on outdated twentieth-century models, will be reorganized to deal with 2020 realities.

Looking Back

Early in this book I promised to tell you about the converged future and how we would get there.

I made the pretty strong claim that convergence was about networks. And that Internet Protocol was the basis for the largest, most powerful, and most efficient community network the human race has ever known. I believe the journey we've gone on, from IP all the way to the converged future, has at least sketched the trajectory we're taking toward full convergence.

Let's review my explanation from Chapter 1:

> *Billions of devices, from temperature sensors to clock radios to cars to supercolliders – connected over extreme broadband to powerful distributed processing, large storage, and intelligent decision-making systems – will create, in the next decade or so, a convergence of communities of technological interest. They will cooperate, gathering resources, performing actions, forming and reforming according to want and need. And*

they'll do it faster and more powerfully than traditional human community networks ever could before.

These communities will wrap intelligence around all our familiar environments – our homes, our cars, our markets and theaters and cities. We will live, fully immersed, within communities of interest that are wider and more powerful than any we have ever known. The future of your business rides on the creation of this grander, richer global network.

This vision, as we've seen throughout the book, is almost a reality. So what could affect your safe arrival in this converged future?

Forces of Control

We discussed how the IP community network was gradually enfolding all forms of communication and media into itself. And I've given you some specific advice during our journey about how to adapt to and cope with this change. With the IP network we have the dynamic, open, and vibrant basis for all future networking. It's about community. And while you might adopt the form of old-school networks for a short time or for a specific application – a broadcast model, or a simple peer-to-peer network – these forms will always be delivered in the context of a larger IP community network. They will not persist or perform in any other form.

The forces of control take many shapes. Sometimes they are the vestiges of old-style networks or legacy systems. Often they are antiquated networks themselves – old, inflexible, closed, proprietary networks. They can be technological in nature, but often they are not; outmoded ways of organizing your human networks are forces of control, too. They are always about habit, comfort, laziness, and familiarity. They're about a lack of imagination. They're about trying to control network resources from the top down, instead of adapting to the lightning-speed innovations of 2020.

The forces of control hold your business back.

In order to propel your business successfully into the future you need to embrace the forces of freedom – networks and structures that allow your company the flexibility to compete in the converged network of 2020. After reading this book, the risks involved in holding on to forces of control should be obvious. Holding on to them is a sure way to guarantee that your business won't arrive in the future we've just explored. Because another company – another CIO – will leverage the flexibility and dynamism of the converged world, and your business will be left in the dust.

The message is, Be flexible. Be prepared.

Flexible Business Networks

We've seen how convergence is widening, disrupting, and transforming the community of networks that make up our world. In the course of these transformations, traditional networks are being destroyed, created, and merged in new and unexpected forms. Your business is just one network within this converging world. Many new demands, engendered by the IP revolution, are being placed on your business. And if your networks are static – based around the forces of control – convergence will grind them up.

Your company needs to be built out of efficient, powerful networks capable of delivering required services to your customers and resources to your employees. These networks have to evolve as quickly as the need for them arises. They need to be available to all your employees and business partners everywhere. And they need to be disbanded as soon as the need is met so their resources can be used fruitfully elsewhere.

What can you do to create these powerful service networks? How can you adjust your technological efforts to leverage the forces of freedom?

Here are some of the key principles you need to keep in mind:

Scale matters. Be ready to serve millions of requests and translate them to billions of sessions where maintaining the full state of these requests is critical. Existing and potential customers alike are surrounded by networks of every conceivable variety, offered by many different providers. These users access these networks over an increasingly diverse array of devices provided by many different companies. You need to leverage this diversity of interconnections to extend your presence to new customers. With this flood of new users and devices, it is necessary to build an IP services infrastructure that can freely and flexibly accept millions of sessions per second.

Of course, you might expect someone in the communications business to tell you this, but the simple truth is that the business of the future is going to succeed (or not) depending on the ability of its IP networks and services to scale for sophisticated collaboration.

Exploit infinite resources. Traditional commodities like bandwidth and storage will become, for all intents and purposes, virtually infinite and relatively inexpensive. How can you adapt and expand your services to leverage this kind of power? Don't let storage and bandwidth limitations *now* dictate your service or network vision for *then*. New network needs, services, and efficiency-enhancing devices are created every day, and you should be poised to take advantage of them.

Even if your services to users don't fundamentally change, the number of potential transactions that are heading your way will be multiplying enormously over the coming years, as the IP network engulfs traditional, centrally controlled business networks.

Compete collaboratively. Instead of creating confusion and frustration among your customers by having an all-out tug-of-war for them, collaborate with your competition in community networks designed to serve your customers better. Initiate joint ventures with your competitors to provide business packages of the highest value for customers. In the end, it isn't about who gets to the customer first, it's about who can serve the customer best. If working collaboratively with your competition provides superior service, everyone will win.

Leverage partnerships. Your customers and their business partners are a differential advantage for your business. Imagine and institute community networks based around them. Old-fashioned vertical business silos are forces of control – they will keep you locked into a linear service mentality. Think horizontally. For example, if you're a manufacturer, consider all your suppliers. Who are they allied with? What sort of services are they offering (or being offered) across their telecommunications networks? How can you incorporate these services into the design of your products? Into the manufacturing process itself? When you build community networks, every member makes the whole more powerful at a staggering rate.

Open up. Use open platforms to create your network and services. Whenever possible, opt for open platforms to create services within transparent, flexible, and scaleable architectures. Open-platform solutions can be integrated quickly, fixed more easily, and customized more specifically to your customers' needs. Proprietary solutions are notorious forces of control – they will slow us all down as we move into the converged network world. Be prepared for tighter integration and standardization within technologies that have never been standardized before – even protocols, hardware, and software.

Be transparent. Concealing routine data is just as costly as sharing confidential data. You and your customers are equal partners in a community of interest. Just as IP helps you become more informed about the needs, habits, and preferences of your customers, your customers will leverage the same technology to understand *you*. There will be more and more data about the quality and price of your products and services at their disposal. They will be able to track your performance just as efficiently as you track theirs. Acknowledge this by being as flexible and open with them about your practices and pricing as you can afford to be. They will be well informed enough to make sound comparisons between you and your competition and, more important, between the level of service you offered in the past and the service you're offering them now. And they will hold you accountable for it.

Platforms for Success

Individual businesses can make wise decisions based on the ideas outlined above. But without active participation by the entire business community – and more particularly, the information technologists within that community – even the best-laid plans can and will fail. How can we focus our efforts as a community network so that we flourish as a whole? And how do we guarantee that our customers and consumers realize the maximum benefit from our efforts?

As we all know, a well-designed platform is a key element of success in the development of any high-tech application. Design your platform well, and your applications will run smoothly; design the platform *really* well, and developers will flock to produce many different and useful applications for it. Platforms are comparatively simple structures that enable innovative services at a higher level of complexity. Similarly, the business community can create "platforms" for flexible networks that mesh with, and enhance, the converged world. As a community, it is in our best interest to foster the forces of freedom at the most fundamental, architectural level. We need simple operating structures within industry that reduce confusion, scatter and share control, make our group efforts more efficient, and encourage competition that is focused on innovative service.

Here are a few additional corporate challenges to help us foster cooperative values in our business and community networks as we approach the converged world.

Help develop global standards. Diversity without standards is chaos; diversity *with* standards is competition. Designers and technologists need help in making the network tools and interoperability of network services universal: protocols, hardware, software, and even the architectures of the networks themselves. The main avenue for convergence among these areas is the creation of globally based open standards. All these technologies must be the product of joint research and development, not "silos" of control that perpetuate proprietary networks. For flexibility to grow, standards of communication and behavior must be established. If all our concerns are on the table, the community will make design decisions that will help all of us flourish.

Foster the education of "converged" engineers. When it comes to technology education, there are fundamental divisions between electrical engineering, which creates devices, and computer engineering, which creates software. The nexus of these two is where the future of the network will be shaped. We need to train engineers and provide them with the skills to bridge disciplines without losing the depth of knowledge in the individual disciplines themselves; they must become converged engineers, possessing computer, electrical, and network engineering skills and uniting these now separate engineering communities. If we don't bridge this gap, we are placing significant roadblocks before businesses in the converged world.

One program I've been involved in that is dedicated to producing just such young technologists is the University of California, San Diego, Center for Network Systems. Hopefully, other programs like this one will be created and nurtured.

Develop and invest in digital rights management (DRM). I know this may sound like a force of control, but networks are nothing without content. People and organizations who create content must be fairly compensated or content will not be created. Napster was a good technology but a poor business model. Apple's iPod is a great technology and a great business model for Apple and the content providers. This migration of movies and music to IP networks is already proving to be an immense boost to economic growth; however, ensuring the integrity of intellectual property is vitally important for this growth to take hold. DRM-enabled IP networks would guarantee that the fruits of creativity would be enjoyed by everyone, with proper credit and recompense given to the creators of multimedia entertainment. If the products and services promised to customers can be copied and stolen by third parties and offered as their own, the incentive for production and creativity is greatly reduced. I believe DRM is a necessary base asset, just like standards; without DRM, content sharing is chaos; content sharing with DRM creates long-term viable business competition.

The Big Picture

Businesses alone cannot ensure the growth and development of the converged world. Society as a whole needs to take steps to create flexibility and openness in the networks of the future. Here are the topline social issues I see for creating a free and open 2020 world.

Educate the legal community. Numerous legal problems and court cases have made evident how low the level of technical sophistication among our elected officials, judges, and legal workers is. To ensure intelligent regulation, public officials must be trained to understand technology – if not on a purely technical level, at least in terms of general systems and models. We cannot rely on short-term technological education in a crisis situation. Lawsuits involving technology rights and intellectual property cannot be judged by juries or jurists who do not understand the basics. Technology law must be developed and nurtured as a discipline, starting with required basic technology education in pre-law programs. The more members of the legal community are educated, the less likely those with specialized knowledge can take advantage of the uneducated.

Beyond that, there's a social and ethical dimension as well. We need elected officials and judges who are well informed about technology and can help explain and fight for the privacy and economic rights of the community as a whole. They should also be capable of explaining comprehensibly the issues at hand to their constituents.

Educate the layperson. Not just public officials, but the layperson – the nontechnical citizen – must, to the best of his or her ability, be trained in the basics of technology, its uses, and its implications. Just as general courses on responsible citizenship are required for our children, we should demand that the responsible uses and applications of technology be taught. Citizens themselves should be given the tools to judge the ethical and economic implications of the technology put into their hands; they will also need information to hold their representatives accountable for their decisions.

Make the "edge" inclusive. One way to ensure network power is to make the development of the network as inclusive as possible. We need to engage in an active cultivation of users and designers from remote or underpriveledged areas, for two important reasons that directly affect network power. First, we've seen how an increase in the number of community members increases the network's power. Second, and more important, the integration of these same users has a cumulative ethical effect. The fewer outsiders there are, the less violent or malicious intrusions are likely to be, thereby helping to ensure network security and integrity.

Beyond these concerns lie questions of economic opportunity and political access, both of which will depend increasingly on access to and knowledge of technology. The telephone system in the United States is a triumph of inclusiveness; the telephone network was far more valuable because it was universal. We need to ensure that as many citizens as possible are able to participate in the network so that inequalities can be easily surmounted by aptitude and skill, rather than the accident of access. The converged world needs to be free and open to all who will use it responsibly.

Create ethical technologists. The future of high technology won't simply require multitalented engineers. It will require the marriage of technical expertise with a larger social vision. On the simplest level this means technologists who are acquainted with or, better yet, multidisciplinary in the fields of law, economics, and business administration. But it also implies an education in political science as well as some experience with the arts. None of the challenges I've outlined in this chapter will be met without technologists like these. Because in the final analysis technology is a branch of science, but the creative application of technology to human life is an art.

Invest in the Future Think about all the benefits the Internet has brought to the economy of both the United States and the world. Thirty-five years ago the seeds of the Internet were sown at the Defense Advanced Research Projects Agency (DARPA); within an astoundingly short period of time the way we approach our lives has been altered in every fundamental way. What will the next technological "big bang" be? The breakthrough technology that fosters economic growth and social revolution for the next thirty-five years? Serious investment in research and development – dedicated funds for theoretical research in a genuinely scientific environment – may spawn technologies that carry the same importance, if not more, than the Internet does today.

Finally, ensure the privacy of the citizen. I maintained in Chapter 3 that the advent of sensor technologies, while the most visible symbol of privacy infringement concerns, was not the most important or pressing issue. The important decisions about maintaining privacy for the citizen lie in the aggregation and use of personal data. While very few sensors have the power, range, or intelligence to track an individual in *1984,* Orwellian style, large-scale databases filled with consumer data can allow for very efficient profiling of individuals. These databases, in the wrong hands, are a very real threat to privacy. Along with enforcing responsible protection of consumer data internally, the sharing of the data among institutions should be approved by the consumer. Without trust in the network, what would the point of having it be?

The Soul of the Network

A crucial service philosophy for a network provider to adopt is, *Build the service around the users.* Don't make them fight to get it. Networks should exist to serve the customer, not the other way around.

As we've seen, it's coming – it's almost here. Step by step, layer by layer, we're watching it rise around us. And in its most ideal form, it develops freely into a converged world network, with the human being at the center of a huge arena that enables collaboration, creativity, and purposeful action on vast scales and at instantaneous speeds. Many of the beautiful dreams of science fiction and futurist thinkers are on the brink of becoming real.

Turning the network inside out demands that we hold one value paramount above the rest: respect for the human beings at its center. Services should be at the disposal of their interests, their needs, their creativity. But how do we ensure that the network that will soon surround us all serves us, and not the other way around?

It's back to the forces of control.

Who controls the network? Is it a common enterprise, forged by business, consumers, and the government, weighing the best interests of each for the free advancement of all? Or will it be controlled by a narrow few, subject to little or no authority or oversight, denying access at a whim? Decisions about the scope and use of the converged world network need to be made by participants in our first, most important, most primary network: the human cultural network and the democracy and freedom that are its grandest expression.

No one person, company, or organization should be given too much control. This is the first step toward engineering values into the network. The future could be a dream come true; but to prevent the opposite, the network must be built in the spirit of providing the greatest material and intellectual freedom to the greatest number of users. We need to try, to the best of our ability, to make sure that none of our fellow humans are left "on the edge." The converged world should be a common enterprise.

On a more fundamental level, we need to maximize the control each user has over his or her participation in the infrastructure itself. The converged world network must always allow the user enough room to be able to consider its value. And it must be built in such a way that we have the space to change it or remove ourselves from it if we think it's necessary for our happiness. We should never become so dependent on technology that we can't have a debate about its value. Otherwise, we will be swept along by our own inventiveness toward an uncertain end.

To avoid these scenarios – to make our converged world live up to all the promise I've outlined in this book – we must engineer it with *respect for ourselves and each other.* And with that sort of respect at the center of our relationships, we can help ensure that the future is the flexible, powerful, liberating environment it should be. In the spirit of that respect, it isn't my job to dictate my values to you. Instead, it's my job – as a businessperson, technologist, and citizen – to initiate, honestly and enthusiastically, conversations about the values we share.

The converged world is coming. What do you want to do with it?

Afterword
2020 Search Technologies

Information overload is nothing new. As long as we have been recording information, we have been inventing ways to retrieve it. The Hittites added title page details to documents back in the thirteenth century BCE. Pliny the Elder, in the year 77, included a table of contents and a bibliography in his landmark work, *Natural History*. Even ancient libraries classified their scrolls and tablets. By the year 1500, with more than nine million printed books in circulation – about the size in terabytes of the print collection of today's Library of Congress – medieval librarians had developed new classification systems to organize knowledge.

Today the amount of information available to us on the World Wide Web is truly extraordinary. You can find everything – the full text of Cicero's speeches to the Roman Senate, the lyrics of a Cole Porter tune, a photograph of the Grand Canal, a repair manual for a 1967 Chevy, a lecture series on the history of jazz complete with audio files and video. Search engines, portals, and online directories constantly innovate with improved search algorithms, new techniques for locating nontextual resources, and the bundling of related applications such as online shopping and communications services. But as the World Wide Web continues to expand the amount and diversity of its information resources, it is evermore challenging to efficiently find what you're looking for.

Formatting an efficient search query can still take a lot of experience or willingness to experiment. As Web searchers, we typically don't spend very much time in seeking an answer; often we don't look beyond the first page of search results. Few of us bother to learn the command structures and more advanced features that will help refine a query, or try out some of the newer services that creatively organize search results.

Creative innovations are helping to refine search results, both simplifying and hastening the search process. Some search interfaces allow you to dynamically modify the parameters of your search by moving "sliders" up or down a scale to add or reduce the importance of certain ranking factors, thereby refining your search. The visual presentation of search results offers the alternative of seeing relationships in the various subtopics related to a search result, thus facilitating browsing. Tagging can improve speed in locating new information on topics interest. By 2020 we will most likely look back at these innovations and see that they were just incremental improvements, compared to what will be possible then.

Using Natural Language

As Web searchers, we are familiar with the "and," "if," and "or" of Boolean searching and the use of keywords to find what we want. The more adventurous use a search engine's special features to set the parameters of what is wanted, such as data in an Excel spreadsheet or information from a recently updated website. Most search engines use natural language processing to handle queries, so we can also try entering a query in the form of a question. However, the quality of results from entering a query in natural language can vary dramatically with the type of question and the search engine used.

In the future, searchers will routinely enter their queries in the form of a question or a statement just as they would speak to another human being. The search technology will be able to parse the query to determine what is needed and will be able to deal with quite complex questions that may require accessing a wide variety of different sources with multiple media types. Instead of entering a list of keywords, searchers will speak conversationally, with questions such as "Is there a Greek restaurant nearby?" or "What killed the dinosaurs?" Or type in statements such as "Find me a recording of Beethoven's Trio in B Flat by the group that played at Carnegie Hall last night."

Future search systems are likely to include an interactive component using natural language questioning that will query the searcher in order to limit the universe of possible data sources and provide greater precision in the final results. When asked a question such as "What happens when a comet hits the earth? the system may ask in turn "Any comet or one large enough to cause major destruction?" A complex question such as "What roots of modern economic theory can be traced to the Scottish Enlightenment?" could result in the reply "Would you like to focus on the theories of Adam Smith?"

The technology underlying the search interface will include sophisticated reasoning systems that can make inferences from the searcher's situation and from the system's collective experience. The search system will be able to build on its accumulated knowledge just as human beings make judgments based on their own lifetime experiences and observations. It will respond to new questions based on previous search requests as well as derive meaning from associated experiences. The automated reasoning process will include the ability to differentiate commonly accepted fact from opinion and to reason the appropriate level of detail needed to sufficiently answer the searcher's query.

Search systems will be able to judge from the form and subject of the question, as well as from other interactions with the questioner, as to what level of detail is needed and the best way to format the answer. A query such as "List the key symptoms of type-2 diabetes" is likely to require a more sophisticated answer than the query "Who are the Seven Sisters?" sent from a cell phone. Search systems will be able to make judgments as to the questioner's intent. From a query such as "What are the safest midsized cars?" the system would conclude that the searcher is likely to be in the market for a new car and include a list ranked by price of cars for sale near her home.

Future search systems will also be far more sophisticated in how they present the results of a query. Rather than producing a ranked list of sources, the search engine will detail an answer to a simple question or will summarize the results in a report organized by clusters of information and sources on different aspects of the topic. At this point the searcher will be able to ask additional questions, purchase an item, make a call to a listed expert, share the results with a group, or merge the information with another document.

Adding Context

Future generations of search technology will also add a richer contextual component to the search process. In addition to assisting us in expressing what we want to find, they will be able to identify our level of interest and expertise, derive how information should best be presented, and infer how we will access it.

Eventually search systems will make use of sensors that will automatically associate information points to present answers in the context of our past activities, interests, and other aspects of our lives. A query regarding an audio recording might result in the system reminding us that we might already own a copy, as it is listed on the CD inventory we maintain on our entertainment hub at home. The search system will be able to correlate a question about diving equipment to past purchases of similar items as birthday gifts for a relative and will automatically provide the date when the item should be shipped in order to arrive before he blows out the candles.

We are seeing early examples of information presented in context with some of today's mobile searching capabilities. Cell phone users, for example, can access Web pages specifically designed for the screen of a handheld device. Most general purpose search systems have local search services where users can find information related to a specific city or zip code. Users can search for restaurants, stores, and other businesses in a specific area, obtain driving directions and maps, and sometimes use a click-to-dial feature to make a telephone call. Users can even bypass Web searching altogether by sending and receiving queries by short message service (SMS).

Search services in the future will automatically be able to discern the best way query results should be delivered. They will know whether we are at home talking to a friend or working on a project in the office, for they will have the ability to reason from whatever limited information we or the ambient circumstances provide. They will be able to postulate scenarios of possible meaning and intent and, by using commonsense reasoning, automatically present results. They will be able to discern information about a questioner's background from her accent or use of variant spelling and combine this knowledge with her current location to present information in context. Shopping information might be presented in dollars and euros if a Glaswegian is asking a question about raincoats from a location in Maine. The response to a question about what is playing in London theaters would be predicated on other interactions indicating that the inquirer is on vacation in England and is fond of Jacobean literature.

By 2020 search systems will be able to make quite sophisticated contextual inferences. Search technologies will have developed far beyond the mere ability to take into account geographic location or personal preferences – they will make inferences based on perceived emotion, cultural perspective, level of topical knowledge, and more. A query about local hospitals might result in driving directions and a click-to-dial 911 button in response to the tension perceived in the questioner's voice. In response to a question about flight schedules, a search system will be able to discern from ambient noise that we are at the airport and will adjust the data presentation accordingly. Future search systems will make correlations among a wide range of data points and our accumulated electronic history. Recipes will be translated into grams for a transplanted European baking a cake in Canada. From past experience, a search system will be able to judge that an inquirer can read classical Latin but will need translations for sources in ecclesiastical Latin. An inquiry about batting averages sent from Yankee Stadium in the middle of the World Series will receive a quite different answer than one from a fourth-grader working on her math homework.

Tomorrow's Search

By the year 2020, search as we know it today will be an anachronism. We won't connect to a website to search for information; instead services will incorporate search capabilities. Information agents will be embedded into these services and will answer questions, make suggestions, update us on past queries, and provide us with reminders. They will anticipate our needs based on our personal preferences and the tasks we are engaged in.

When we do conduct a search for information, instead of entering keyword queries into a search interface and sifting through a list of static links, we will interactively converse with information agents that will proactively compile data from multiple sources. The search system will use its reasoning capabilities to comprehend what we are requesting and how to deliver the answer. Boolean logic will once again be rel-egated to algebra class.